firstfoods

first foods

**Expert advice and easy recipes by
dietitians for parents of 6–24 month olds**

Includes
recipes with
an Asian
flavour

• Anna Jacob • Pauline Chan • Samantha Thiessen
• Janie Chua • Wong Yuefen

Marshall Cavendish
Editions

Editor   : Lydia Leong

Designer   : Lynn Chin Nyuk Ling

Photographer : Joshua Tan, Elements By The Box

First published 2007
Reprinted 2008, 2009

Published by Marshall Cavendish Cuisine
An imprint of Marshall Cavendish International
1 New Industrial Road, Singapore 536196

Other Marshall Cavendish Offices:

Marshall Cavendish Ltd. 5th Floor, 32–38 Saffron Hill, London EC1N 8FH, UK • Marshall Cavendish Corporation. 99 White Plains Road, Tarrytown NY 10591-9001, USA • Marshall Cavendish International (Thailand) Co Ltd. 253 Asoke, 12th Flr, Sukhumvit 21 Road, Klongtoey Nua, Wattana, Bangkok 10110, Thailand • Marshall Cavendish (Malaysia) Sdn Bhd, Times Subang, Lot 46, Subang Hi-Tech Industrial Park, Batu Tiga, 40000 Shah Alam, Selangor Darul Ehsan, Malaysia

Marshall Cavendish is a trademark of Times Publishing Limited

National Library Board Singapore Cataloguing in Publication Data

First foods : expert advice and easy recipes by dietitians for parents of 6-24 month olds /
Anna Jacob ... [et al.]. – Singapore : Marshall Cavendish Editions, c2007.
p. cm.
Includes index.
ISBN-13 : 978-981-261-334-9
ISBN-10 : 981-261-334-X

1. Infants – Nutrition. 2. Toddlers – Nutrition. 3. Baby foods.
4. Cookery (Baby foods) I. Jacob, Anna, 1962-

RJ216
649.3 -- dc22   SLS2007023433

Printed in Singapore by KWF Printing Pte Ltd

contents

acknowledgements

We would like to thank everyone who contributed to this book in one way or another:

Dr Roy Joseph for writing the foreword to this book.

Li Yuin for editing the text, coordinating the photoshoot and taking care of the finer aspects of the publication of this book.

Amy, Alexandria and Joycelyn, our colleagues at Food and Nutrition Specialists Pte Ltd, for walking with us through the creation of the book and giving us their invaluable suggestions on the content and recipes.

The babies of our colleagues — Jensen, Ian and Jobyn — for patiently tasting our kitchen creations time and time again without complaining!

Babies Elena, Ernest, Gareth, Kiera, Kirsten, Marissa, Peter, Renee, Ryan, Xixi, Zhiyu and Zoe for being our beloved models. Also, special thanks to the parents and grandparents who supported the babies through the hectic photoshoot.

Lydia, our editor, for inviting us to create this special book and working with us through the long gestational process.

Lynn, the designer, for adding colour and style to the book.

Joshua and Julian, the photographers, who made the recipes and the people come to life with their creativity.

Marshall Cavendish International (Asia) Private Limited, our publisher, for the opportunity to make our dreams come true with the publication of *First Foods* and our next endeavour — a recipe book for feeding older children.

All our family members and friends who were very supportive throughout the creative process.

foreword

A major factor that promotes health in a child is the emotional and physical well-being produced by an appropriate feeding programme. This requires parents to have at least a basic understanding of nutritional principles and their application to produce safe, tasty, appealing and balanced meals, offered in a conducive and tension-free setting, and in appropriate amounts.

In my experience as a paediatrician, about a third of the parents who seek consultation at my practice have major gaps in the knowledge and/or skills relating to feeding their infants. It is common during a medical consultation that the majority of the time is spent in discussing feeding issues. I believe this is the same with most paediatricians.

Most of today's young parents would have grown up in small nuclear families and not have had the opportunity to witness the preparation of food and the manner of feeding infants and toddlers. Their primary source of information is likely to be from magazines, the Internet and advice (often conflicting) from family and friends. They are given plenty of fish and sometimes even the rod and line, but never taught how to fish.

First Foods takes pains to teach the reader how to fish and everything beyond, including providing what is usually absent — local knowledge. This is what makes this book unique. Its authors have provided scientific principles and translated them into relevant applications. They have also used their personal experiences to produce in just sufficient amounts, simple, economical, practical and tested solutions to enable each feed to become physically and emotionally satisfying, and a memorable experience for both the child and parent.

The use of the first person setting, illustrations and colour, text boxes for tips and salient points and the avoidance of technical words and jargon is a sure recipe for success. Read, study and follow, and I am sure a happy, thriving baby and a satisfied and empowered parent will emerge.

Roy Joseph, MBBS, MMed (Pead), FRCPH
Senior Consultant, Department of Neonatology, NUH
Associate Professor in Paediatrics, Yong Loo Lin School of Medicine, NUS

introduction

Feeding babies is an age old craft, yet it often raises concern and even anxiety among new parents. Mums and dads worry about what to feed their precious little one, how best to do it and how much baby needs to eat to stay healthy and grow well.

Parents delve through baby books, listen to parenting talks, search the Internet, and talk with their family members and friends just to get some guidance on how to feed their baby right. To add complexity to the situation, in recent years, many new nutrients have been discovered, while new roles and functions of well-established ones have been uncovered. Nutritional guidance for infants and babies has also been revised by international and national health agencies to protect the health of children. With so much information out there, how can a parent decide what is current and reliable?

Living in Asia, new parents have a rich heritage of child feeding traditions and they also receive an abundance of advice from well-meaning and experienced family members. All of this needs to be taken into consideration when deciding what and when to feed their baby. It is not surprising that many mums and dads would certainly appreciate more clarity in this area!

We wrote *First Foods* to explain current food and nutrition information in a simple and practical manner to help parents feed their babies and toddlers with more confidence. As a team of dietitians, we not only share our knowledge, training and experiences, but also answer the concerns of the many parents we have met in our years of practice.

This book lays out the nutrition basics so first time mums and dads can get a better understanding of baby's nutritional needs through the first two years of life. We have also created delicious and nutritious recipes for your little wonder. To meet the needs of modern parents, we took a multicultural approach to our recipes and have included a fantastic mix of delicious and easy recipes from different cuisines that are suitable for each stage of baby's development.

Using our recipes and meal planner, you can be assured that your baby will be well nourished, while enjoying a wide repertoire of foods and flavours. Each of our recipes was created for a nutritional reason, but every one of them was also tested and re-tested by our team to ensure that the final dish tastes good and is easy to prepare. Some of our recipes will also give your child the opportunity to taste, experience and form an opinion about individual foods, such as sweet potatoes, pumpkins and avocados.

Remember, eating is a necessity as well as a pleasure. As parents, you have the joy and privilege to introduce your baby to the wonderful world of food. Guiding your baby's food choices will help ensure that your baby has a healthy attitude towards food and eating. We passionately believe that allowing your child to learn to eat independently as early as possible will help him/her develop a greater interest in food and build up confidence. It will also go a long way towards relieving excessive pressure on yourselves and/or your child's caregivers during mealtimes. This book aims to help you raise a child with the essential skills of self-feeding, and the confidence to explore new tastes and textures with joy.

We have used the generic 'he' throughout this book when referring to the baby or toddler simply for ease of reference. All the information and recipes in this book are suitable for both male and female babies.

Anna Jacob

ready, get set, go!

basic nutrition information to get you started

Basic Nutrition Information to Get You Started

The first year of life is the fastest growth period. It is fascinating that babies generally double their birth weight during the first six months, and triple it by the time they are one year old. Just imagine that! At no other period in an individual's life, does one grow at such a rate. Well-fed babies will meet the nutritional demands of their bodies to fuel and support this amazing phase of life.

All healthy, full-term babies have essentially the same nutritional needs. Babies start off with the same food — milk, and it is the transition from exclusive milk feeds to the addition of solid foods that can be confusing. Fear not, you are not alone! But, before you start cooking, it is important to understand your baby's nutritional needs.

Breastfeeding, the Best Beginning

Nature knows best, that is why breastfeeding is the ideal sole source of nutrition for newborn babies. Authorities like the World Health Organization (WHO) and national health promotion agencies encourage mothers to breastfeed their infants exclusively for six months and then, continue to breastfeed for two years or more.

Breast milk is the ideal food for growing babies because its composition is unique. Breast milk and breastfeeding provide many benefits for babies and mothers too.

Benefits for Baby

- Breast milk provides all the nutrients babies need in the first six months of life. The composition of breast milk also changes to suit the needs of growing babies. Breast milk contains unique fat components such as docosahexaenoic acid (DHA) and arachidonic acid (AA) that are now recognised to help with brain and eye development.

- Human breast milk is custom-made for the human infant and so, it is easily digested and absorbed.

- Breast milk is packed with growth factors, enzymes and immune system components that help babies to grow well and fight diseases. When a mother begins breastfeeding, breast milk is thick and yellow. This first milk, called colostrum, is rich in immune factors that line your baby's mucous membranes helping to guard against disease-causing germs. Breastfed babies also tend to have fewer incidences of diarrhoea, respiratory illnesses and ear infections.

- Breastfed babies have a lower risk of developing allergies.

Did You Know?
Breast milk's nutrient composition changes from the beginning to the end of a feed. The beginning of the feed tends to be thin and watery to quench baby's thirst, while the end of the feed is higher in fat to satisfy baby's hunger.

- Breastfeeding may boost baby's intelligence. Scientific studies have demonstrated that babies breastfed six months or longer have the greatest advantage.
- Breastfed babies are least likely to become obese later on in life as they are better at regulating their feeding.

Benefits for Mum

- Believe it or not, breastfeeding is convenient! Once breastfeeding is established, breast milk is always available and at the right temperature too. So, you can feed your baby anytime, anywhere. To top it off, parents and other caregivers will be glad for reduced washing and sterilising of feeding bottles and paraphernalia!
- Breastfeeding is nature's special way of helping a mother establish a strong bond with her baby that is the very foundation for their future relationship, and something no one else can share. Mums, do cherish the time spent feeding your baby!
- Breastfeeding helps mothers lose the weight gained during pregnancy more easily. Breastfeeding may also reduce a mother's risk of developing some types of cancer.

With so much to go for breastfeeding, every mother should initiate and try to sustain breastfeeding. So, mothers, if you want to breastfeed successfully, eat well and be motivated and patient. Enjoy a varied, balanced diet, drink plenty of fluids and do not overly restrict food intake. All of this will help you to produce enough milk to nourish your baby. Rest assured that you will still be able to lose the weight gained during your pregnancy even though you are eating and drinking more during this period than when you were pregnant.

Real Mum Tip: If you have breastfeeding problems, get a lactation consultant in your maternity hospital to help you. They will be able to provide good advice and also reassurance — something every mother can use!

Bottle Feeding, Your Next Best Option

Breastfeeding is strongly encouraged, but it is up to you to decide whether it is best for you and your baby. Bottle feeding is usually discouraged until after four to six weeks of age due to "nipple confusion". This simply means that a newborn baby may become confused between breast and bottle when offered nipples of different sizes and shapes. This may result in rejection of one or the other and potentially lead to feeding problems.

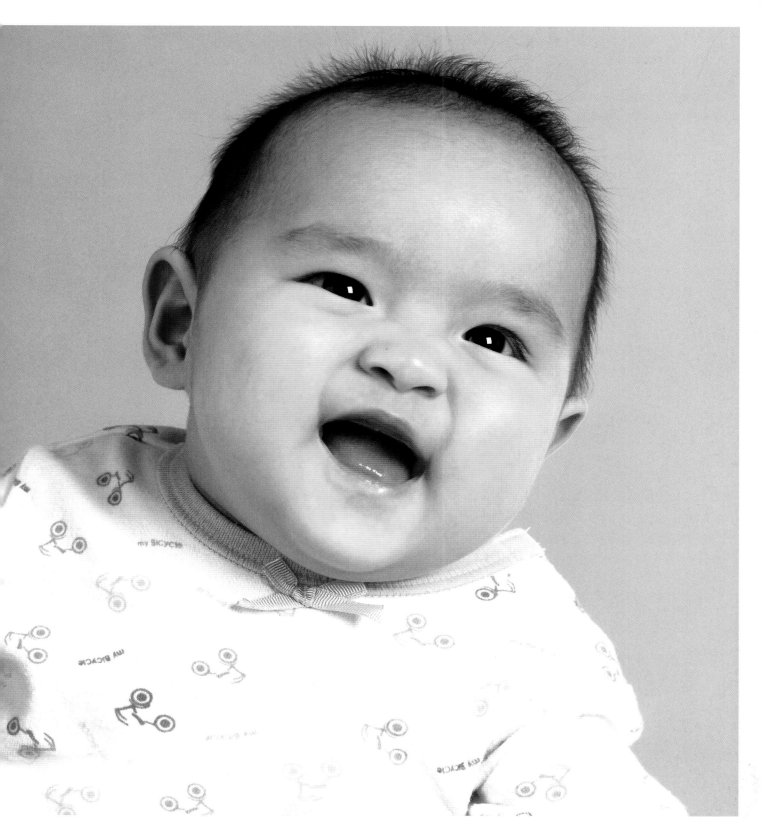

Bottle feeding can be done in addition to breastfeeding, by expressing breast milk with a pump. In many cases, this gives dad the opportunity to bond with the baby and allows mum to rest. If you are unable to, or choose not to breastfeed, perhaps for medical reasons, speak to your child's paediatrician or GP about a recommendation for a suitable feeding alternative. Infant formula, whether soy or cow's milk-based, is specially formulated to be safe and nutritionally adequate for babies, and should be used as recommended by the doctor. Do not use regular cow's milk to replace breast milk, as it is not equivalent nutritionally, and may trigger allergies and gastro-intestinal distress in babies.

Safety Tip: If your baby does not finish a whole bottle of milk, you must discard the leftover to prevent spoilage by germs and enzymes from baby's mouth.

The Nutrition Basics

How much do you really know about nutrition? We all need good nutrition, but our needs vary. Here is a breakdown of the essential nutrients in our diets, and how they relate to a baby's nutritional needs. This should give you the foundation to better understand your baby's needs. You do not, however, need to worry about fitting each and every nutrient into your baby's diet. You can achieve good nutrition for your baby by offering a wide variety of foods in the right proportions for each stage of growth. We will guide you through each chapter, designed for your baby's age, and explain how your baby's changing needs will be met with a variety of foods.

Water

Although water does not provide any calories, it is essential for the body's daily functioning. Breastfed babies will not require extra fluid for approximately the first six months, as breast milk will provide adequate fluids. Breastfed babies get any extra fluid they need by feeding longer or more often. Drinking water will, in fact, affect appetite and reduce suckling.

Most babies fed infant formula also get enough water if they are feeding well, as there is sufficient water in the formula to meet their needs. Remember, however, to use clean, boiled water cooled to lukewarm temperature to prepare infant formula, and follow the mixing instructions carefully.

If you are worried that your baby is suffering from constipation, discuss it with your baby's paediatrician or GP. As long as your baby passes soft stools regularly and painlessly, the bowel movement pattern may be normal.

Some babies, however, need extra fluid in the form of water at certain times, such as during a fever or after profuse sweating. If there is vomiting or diarrhoea, consult the doctor immediately. There may be a need for additional fluid with electrolytes.

Carbohydrates

This is our body's main energy source, and our body and brain work best using this type of fuel.

Carbohydrates are found in abundance in grain foods like rice, bread, pasta, noodles and cereals. Babies should start their eating adventure with the least allergenic grain — rice, and be introduced to different types of grains for variety and good nutrition as they grow older.

Offer your baby whole grains like brown rice and wholegrain bread once he is ready for these foods, as they are more nutritious than refined products like white rice and white bread. However, do not become overzealous and overload your baby's diet with extra fibre by topping up his meals and snacks with high fibre foods such as bran and wheat germ. The excessive fibre will swell in baby's tummy, making him feel full and he will be unable to eat enough to sustain growth.

Carbohydrates are also found in nourishing food choices such as milk, fruit and vegetables. Fruit will be a mainstay of carbohydrates in your baby's diet after introducing rice cereal. Bananas, papayas, watermelons, mangoes, apples and pears will offer your baby the pleasures of natural sweetness, but also come packed with valuable vitamins, minerals and fibre. Root vegetables such as potatoes and carrots are good sources of carbohydrates.

Carbohydrates are also present in table sugar, brown sugar, rock sugar, honey and glucose which are found in many popular foods such as cakes, biscuits and candy. These added sugars provide calories and little else. So, we encourage you to hold off the use of added sugars for the first year and then, only introduce these ingredients in treat foods to be enjoyed occasionally and in moderation.

Best For Your Baby
Milk contains a carbohydrate called lactose which is a great carbohydrate choice for your baby.

Real Mum Tip: A baby's palate is very sensitive and can appreciate the natural tastes of food without the need for added flavourings. Go ahead and taste the foods you prepare for your baby. Do not worry even if it is bland, as your baby will still enjoy it. If it is very tart, however, blend it with a sweet fruit or vegetable, or dilute it with a little pure fruit juice.

Protein

This key nutrient is important for growth and repair of muscles and other tissues in the body. We need an adequate amount to fight disease and maintain a strong immune system. Rich food sources of protein include meat, poultry, fish, eggs, cheese, lentils, tofu and nuts. Your baby will be getting most of his protein from breast milk in the first six to nine months of life, but once your baby is comfortable with eating some solid foods, you can begin to try a variety of meat purées, yoghurt or plant proteins such as tofu and lentils.

Fat

We all need some fat in our diet and babies need more fat per kilogram of body weight than adults. Fat helps with brain and nerve development, and supports baby's rapid growth rate.

All fats, however, are not created equal and each of them has different, but beneficial roles for your baby's growth and health. So, while you may want to cut back on fat to maintain a healthy weight and reduce your risk of certain lifestyle diseases, do not restrict fat in your baby's diet until after the age of two years.

Saturated Fat: Saturated fat is found mostly from animal sources like butter, lard and ghee, with the exceptions being coconut and palm oils. A good rule of thumb to identify saturated fats is that these fats tend to be solid at room temperature. Almost half of the fat in breast milk is saturated. So, while adults are encouraged to eat less saturated fat, you can use these fats sensibly to prepare food for your baby.

Unsaturated Fat: These fats tend to be liquid at room temperature and are derived mostly from plant sources, such as vegetable oils. These oils are recommended as healthier choices for adults. Unsaturated fats make up a little more than half the fat in breast milk and some of them have unique roles that are vital for the optimal growth and development of your baby.

Essential Fatty Acids (EFA): These are a particular type of unsaturated fat that is required by the body, but is not produced by the body. As such, we have to obtain these fatty acids from our diet. They are required by the body in metabolic processes and too little or an incorrect balance can affect baby's development, or cause illness in adults.

Two well-known EFA families include omega-3 fatty acids and omega-6 fatty acids. Linoleic acid and alpha-linolenic acid are well known members of each family. In the body, they form longer chain fatty acids, such as arachidonic acid (AA), docosahexaenoic acid (DHA) and eicosapentaenoic acid (EPA), that have important biological functions.

Some of the food sources of omega-3 fatty acids are canola and soy bean oils, green leafy vegetables, walnuts and fatty fish such as salmon, sardine, tuna, mackerel and anchovies. Omega-6 fatty acids are found in most vegetable oils including corn, soy bean, sunflower, safflower, olive, peanut and canola oils as well as in meat, organ meats, eggs and dairy products.

Breast milk naturally contains DHA, AA and their precursors. The levels found in breast milk reflect the amount of fatty acids a mother consumes in her diet. So, if you are pregnant or breastfeeding, remember to include foods rich in EFAs in your diet, especially the omega-3s.

Trans Fat: Trans fats are primarily found in foods made with hydrogenated fats. Hydrogenation is a process that makes unsaturated liquid oil more solid or more stable. Trans fats have recently come under fire as they are believed to raise "bad cholesterol" levels, which increase the risk of coronary heart disease in adults.

Recent studies have confirmed that trans fats consumed by a pregnant mother will cross the placenta to her growing baby and can be found in her breast milk as well. Trans fats are also naturally found in foods like meat, milk, butter and cheese, but in small amounts. Foods traditionally high in trans fats include cookies, biscuits, pastries, muffins, cakes and some deep-fried foods made with hydrogenated oils. So, these are foods that both you and your little one will need to minimise consumption of.

Vitamins and Minerals

Vitamins and minerals may not provide any energy, but they are essential for growth, development and good health.

Vitamins fall under two categories: water soluble vitamins and fat soluble vitamins. Water soluble vitamins are not stored in the body, so we get what we need from the foods we eat. They tend to be easily damaged by heat (such as during cooking), and include the family of B vitamins and vitamin C. Fat soluble vitamins can be stored in the body. While they are essential for health, consuming large amounts can be toxic. They include vitamins A, D, E and K.

This table is a basic information guide of the key vitamins and minerals in a healthy diet. In general, both adults and infants require the same vitamins and minerals but, of course, babies need much less of each because of their significantly smaller size. Note, however, that it is not necessary to be overly concerned or strict about the daily consumption of each one of these nutrients. Offering babies a healthy and varied diet, will ensure that they are meeting their vitamin and mineral needs.

VITAMIN	WHAT IT DOES...	FOOD SOURCES
A	Boosts immunity Promotes good vision Promotes growth Maintains healthy skin and eyes	Carrots, sweet potatoes, pumpkins, dark green leafy vegetables (such as broccoli, spinach, chye sim and kai lan), yellow and orange-coloured fruit (rock melons, papayas, mangoes), red capsicums, liver, fatty fish (sardines, salmon, tuna and mackerel), milk, egg yolks, cheese
B_1 (Thiamin)	Helps release energy from food Helps with nerve growth, mental function and memory	Pork, liver, soy milk, fortified breakfast cereals, green peas, spinach, corn, oranges, beans, wholegrain cereals (rice and wheat)
B_2 (Riboflavin)	Releases energy from food Promotes growth and development	Liver, dairy products (milk, cheese, yoghurt), fortified breakfast cereals, eggs, dark green leafy vegetables, broccoli

VITAMIN	WHAT IT DOES...	FOOD SOURCES
B_3 (Niacin)	Releases energy from food Involved in many cellular metabolic reactions Maintains healthy cholesterol levels	Liver, chicken, turkey, fatty fish, beef, fortified breakfast cereals, potatoes
Folate	Helps to make new cells including new red blood cells Helps the body make proteins and DNA	Dark green leafy vegetables, broccoli, liver, fortified breakfast cereals, asparagus, broccoli, dried beans and lentils, orange juice
B_{12} (Cobalamin)	Converts folate to active form Important for nerve health and function	Liver, meat, fish, poultry, shellfish, milk, cheese, yoghurt, eggs, tempeh
Vitamin C	Makes collagen to maintain skin elasticity and keep bones strong Helps with wound healing Boosts immunity	Citrus fruit (oranges, grapefruit), strawberries, kiwi fruit, peaches, papayas, dark green leafy vegetables, cabbage, broccoli, capsicums (bell peppers), bean sprouts, tomatoes
Vitamin D	Increases calcium and phosphorus absorption Helps develop and maintain strong teeth and bones	Fatty fish, fortified milk, butter, veal, beef, egg yolks, liver
Vitamin E	Protects cells from damaging free radicals Improves immunity	Fortified breakfast cereals, plant oils (sunflower, soy bean, corn, canola), tofu, orange-coloured vegetables (sweet potatoes, carrots), dark green leafy vegetables, broccoli, liver, egg yolks
Vitamin K	Important for blood coagulation Helps build strong bones	Dark green leafy vegetables, cabbage, broccoli, asparagus, cucumber, liver

Minerals, like vitamins, are important in maintaining baby's optimal growth, development and good health. There are some key minerals that are needed for the formation of bones and blood cells, while other minerals are only needed in small or trace amounts. The following table is a list of key minerals needed for baby's growth and development.

MINERAL	WHAT IT DOES...	FOOD SOURCES
Iron	Essential element of red blood cells Maintains immune system Promotes optimal cognitive development	Iron-fortified baby cereals, red meats (beef, lamb), baked beans, liver, fish, poultry, shellfish, eggs, dried beans or lentils, spinach and enriched bread
Calcium	Formation and maintenance of healthy teeth and bones Role in blood coagulation Helps transmission of nerve impulses and muscle contraction	Dairy products (milk, cheese, yoghurt), dark green vegetables, broccoli, salmon, tofu, fish with edible bones (anchovies (*ikan bilis*), whitebait, fresh and canned sardines), calcium-fortified foods (milk, orange juice, water, breads and biscuits)
Zinc	Maintains immune system Helps cell growth Promotes wound healing Maintains sense of smell and taste	Meats (beef, pork, veal), fish, poultry, dark green vegetables, whole grains (wholemeal bread, brown rice)
Iodine	Promotes growth, development and brain function	Seafood, dairy products, seaweed, iodised salt

Iron is a particularly important mineral for baby's development because it is an essential part of the body's red blood cells. Red blood cells carry oxygen from the lungs to the body tissues through our blood stream. A baby's liver has iron reserves at birth, but this only lasts until baby is six months old. This is why we strongly recommend introducing iron-fortified rice cereal as the first food. Iron-deficiency anemia is a common condition in children and is prevalent in developing nations, particularly in Asian countries. Children who suffer from this type of anemia tend to have stunted growth and a lower intelligence quotient (IQ) level than those without anemia. Iron deficiency can have long-term effects that are usually irreversible. Foods that are rich in vitamin C can help boost the iron absorption from iron-rich foods. Older children, for example, can be served a citrus fruit together with a meal of spinach or beef.

Most of us are familiar with dairy products as important food sources of calcium, but alternative sources also include certain green leafy vegetables. These, however, are less valuable sources of calcium since calcium absorption is affected by the fibre and oxalic acid content in the vegetables.

A good rule of thumb about zinc is that high protein foods tend to be good sources of zinc. Fruit and vegetables are not considered good sources of zinc because the zinc in plant foods is not as readily available for use by the body.

Iodine is a major component of the thyroid hormone which is essential for body growth, development and function, especially that of the brain in fetal and early post-natal life. Iodine deficiency may lead to brain damage and mental retardation. Iodised salt may be the primary food source of iodine in many countries, but it is also widely available in seafood such as cod, sea bass, salmon and shellfish. Dairy products, seaweed and plants grown in soil that is rich in iodine are also good sources of iodine.

Other Nutrients in the News

Many products targeted at mums-to-be and infants seem to have a host of nutrients added to them, causing many parents to feel that these must be better for their infants. We have included a short list of the most popular nutrients included in these products to help you understand their role, and the natural food sources where these nutrients are available, so you can make an informed decision about whether your child needs supplemented products after the age of one.

Choline

Choline plays a vital role in human brain development, and brain, memory and cardiovascular function. It is also important for the composition and repair of cellular membranes. The presence of adequate amounts of choline during pregnancy and breastfeeding ensures healthy fetal brain development that may have long-lasting positive effects on cognitive function, including memory.

Choline is widely distributed in foods. Meat, organ meats such as liver and kidney, wheat germ, leafy vegetables, soy and egg yolks are good sources of choline.

Taurine

Taurine is a natural component of breast milk and is found in higher concentrations in the brain and retina of an infant. Scientists believe that it may have a role in brain formation, vision and hearing. Sources of dietary taurine include shellfish and organ meats such as liver.

Beta-Carotene

This is a form of carotene, a colour pigment that is widely distributed in nature and most efficiently converted to vitamin A by the body. Carotenes produce the orange, yellow and red colours of carrots, tomatoes and oranges.

Sialic Acid

Breast milk is a rich source of sialic acid, a carbohydrate. Sialic acid plays a role in the way cells communicate, especially brain and nerve cells, which impacts memory. Sialic acid may also boost immunity against the influenza (flu) virus.

Selenium

Selenium is a mineral found naturally in breast milk and in a variety of foods such as chicken, tuna, beef, eggs and cheese. Selenium acts as an anti-oxidant in the body, protecting cells from damage.

Real Mum Tip: Do not stress yourself out! You do not need supplements to achieve your healthy baby's nutritional goals. Offer a wide variety of foods each day to ensure your baby gets all the nutrients needed to stay healthy and achieve optimal overall growth.

the food adventure begins

4 to 6 months of age

Introducing Solid Food

The general consensus on when to introduce new and more solid foods into a baby's diet is based on developmental readiness, which should fall somewhere between four and six months of age. The American Academy of Pediatrics (AAP) recommends that babies should not be introduced to other foods apart from breast milk before four months, nor should it be delayed beyond six months of age. This is simply because there is no nutritional need for anything but breast milk before four to six months, and at this stage, babies are also not physically ready to deal with food in a more solid form. However, waiting beyond six months may delay future developmental milestones as well as foster poor acceptance of new foods, tastes and textures. After six months of age, exclusively breastfed babies need other sources of iron, whether it is from food or from iron drops.

There are some clear cues that indicate your baby may be ready for solids. These coincide with progress in baby's physical and mental development that allows transition from sucking to chewing and even, swallowing. Here is what you need to look out for in your baby:

- Seems dissatisfied with milk feeds alone.
- Indicates interest in food that you are eating.
- Shows interest in things around.
- Able to sit with some support.
- Has good control of head and neck.
- Does not push out solid food placed on the tongue.

When your baby is ready for solids, it is an exciting time! Here are some tips to help you get started.

When babies are not ready to eat solid foods, they will push it out even if the food is placed in their mouth. Do not get upset, as they are not making a statement about your cooking!

32

Tips for Feeding

- Get some baby-friendly equipment. Here is what you will need:
  - Plastic spoons for babies.
  - Plastic bowls. Non-slip, stable baby-friendly ones with lids are readily available.
  - Bibs. You will need a few, but avoid ones with ties as they may hurt baby.
  - Highchair, if possible.

- Be patient and do not rush.
  - This is supposed to be a new and enjoyable experience for both you and your baby. Take your time, relax and do not worry if your baby is not taking to these new textures and tastes right away.

- Take advice from friends and family in stride.
  - It is up to you to make the right choice for your baby.

- Choose a time when your baby is hungry but not ravenous.
  - Timing the first meal before a milk feed is ideal, but not if your baby is really hungry. Sometimes it helps to breastfeed or bottle feed a small amount before introducing your baby's first solid food.

- Serving sizes
  - One to two teaspoons may be all your baby wants in the beginning and gradually, this will increase to a quarter of a cup as he gets accustomed to the solids. It is important to note that solid food is not really providing much, if any, nutrition in the beginning, so it is important to keep the same amount of milk feeds as usual.

- Start with simple, basic foods
  - More on this coming up…

First foods are smooth and runny. Start with just one to two teaspoonfuls. Your aim is to encourage your baby to learn to eat.

First Foods

We recommend that a baby's first solid food should always be iron-fortified rice cereal. This is because rice is one of the least allergenic foods and as such, is the ideal first food. After your baby has accepted the rice cereal and shows no adverse reactions, progress to other single ingredient foods (i.e. not combined with other ingredients). We recommend that you start with vegetables, fruit and other grains, before moving on to protein-rich foods such as meat and tofu. Purée each single ingredient to a smooth consistency and add small amounts of breast milk or formula to the purée, if needed, to create a smooth but runny texture.

Why Start with Purées?

Purées are an ideal way to introduce single ingredients to your baby. Feeding single ingredients is crucial to ensure that baby has no allergic reactions to new foods. Each new single ingredient food must be introduced on its own, one at a time, for three days at a stretch, to ensure there is no adverse reaction before moving on to the next food. We also recommend the use of a food diary to help you keep track of the dates and any possible reaction your baby may have to a new food.

In many Asian households, porridges rather than purées are the first foods offered to babies. Parents and caregivers go to great lengths to buy the best and even expensive ingredients to add to the porridge. Much care is taken to cook the porridge over low heat until the final product is very soft and flavourful. Many parents are convinced that it is best to follow this traditional practice, as slow-cooked porridges are very nourishing and easy for baby to eat. As dietitians, however, we believe that many of the precious nutrients in the ingredients are lost through prolonged cooking. In our porridge recipes, we encourage parents to add separately prepared meat and vegetable purées to a basic plain porridge to enhance the nutrient values of the dish. To prove that this makes a difference, we sent samples of a porridge prepared using the two different methods to the laboratory for testing. The results confirmed that the levels of key nutrients were significantly higher for the porridge prepared using our method. It had 24% more protein; 134% more beta-carotene; 100% more vitamin B_2; and 22% more vitamin B_3. With our cooking method, your baby will also be able to savour the taste of the individual ingredients in the porridge rather than a blended flavour of many ingredients.

So, How Does One Start?

There are a few basic things to keep in mind before you put that first spoonful in your baby's mouth. Remember that this is a new and strange experience for your baby, so you need to approach it with a positive and relaxed attitude. Here are some tips to get you and your baby set up for the first meal!

- Start when baby is hungry, but not ravenous.
- Both you and baby should be seated comfortably.
- Minimise distractions. Remove toys and switch off the television.
- Give baby your full attention during the entire feeding process.
- Allow sufficient time to start and complete the task.
- Start with small serving sizes (one to three teaspoons), and offer second helpings if your baby still shows interest.
- Avoid force feeding, even if your baby refuses the food.

There are no hard and fast rules about which vegetable or fruit you should start your baby on first, but from a dietitian's perspective and based on our experience, this is a good guide to help you get started on choosing what to feed your baby.

Vegetables (in no particular order)
- Sweet potatoes
- Pumpkins
- Carrots
- Peas
- Spinach

Fruit (in no particular order)
- Apples
- Pears
- Bananas
- Honeydew or rock melons

Use our recipes and meal planner (pages 152–153) to prepare delicious and healthy meals and snacks for your baby. In the beginning, you will need to feed your baby solids just once a day, in addition to providing all the regular milk feeds. Over time, you can increase the portion of solids and reduce the amount of milk at each feed. Following this, you will need to add on another solid feed, until by the age of 12 months, your baby is eating three meals and having one or two snacks, in addition to milk feeds.

Top 10 Problem Foods
(in alphabetical order)

- Berries (strawberries, raspberries, blueberries)
- Bird's nest
- Cow's milk
- Crustacean shellfish
- Egg white
- Fish
- Peanuts
- Soy
- Tree nuts (almonds, Brazil nuts, cashews, hazelnuts, macadamia nuts, pecans, pine nuts, pistachios, walnuts)
- Wheat

Allergies and Intolerances

There are so many myths and misconceptions about food allergies today. Food allergy is defined by the American Academy of Pediatrics (AAP) as an "immunologic reaction resulting from the ingestion of a food or a food additive". This simply means that your immune system — not your stomach or digestive system — reacts with something (usually protein) in the food.

Food allergies are rare, but can be serious, and the reactions themselves can vary greatly between individuals. The most serious reaction is known as anaphylaxis, which can be life threatening. Symptoms usually include swelling in the mouth and throat, difficulty in breathing and shock. Those with serious food allergies are diagnosed by an allergy specialist physician and often carry around medication in case of accidental ingestion of an offending food.

Many children with food allergies will outgrow them, but some do not. If there is history of food allergy in your family, you want to be especially careful since there is an increased risk that your baby may have food sensitivities or allergies also. Your baby's paediatrician or GP may recommend that you delay the introduction of potentially allergenic foods such as wheat, seafood and cow's milk.

More common are what are known as an "adverse reaction to food" or "food intolerance". Adverse reactions can appear as symptoms similar to food allergies, but the immune system is not involved. Adverse reactions can be caused by food or additives in food, such as colourants or preservatives. Having a food intolerance does not mean an individual is allergic. It usually means that the person lacks enzymes to break down certain food components. A good example is lactose intolerance, where individuals cannot break down the sugar in milk (lactose). Adults who are lactose intolerant can choose lactose-free dairy products or take special lactase pills in order to enjoy regular dairy products.

Write it Down!

Keep a record of the dates you introduce new foods to your baby to help you watch for any possible reactions to new foods. It is a good idea to be extra careful when introducing potentially allergenic foods like wheat, berries and nuts. Note down the new food introduced to your baby and wait three days before moving on to the next food.

Homemade Versus Commercially-prepared Baby Food

Many new mothers feel intimidated by the task of preparing homemade baby food in addition to caring for a young baby. There is no need to be! Cooking for baby can be easy and rewarding. It also allows your baby to get used to the types of food you usually eat as a family, and you can be assured of what it contains. That said, in terms of nutrition, commercially-prepared baby foods compare well with homemade versions. They are convenient, portable and come in a variety of flavours. The choice is endless, and stricter regulations mean they must be lower in sodium.

Nonetheless, parents who prepare homemade baby food are able to offer their children a wide variety of foods that may not be available commercially. We are also big proponents of using fresh ingredients for great taste! As such, we have included easy, practical and delicious recipes drawn from both Asian and Western cuisines to give you a great head start.

Here is a list of the basic equipment you will need for preparing homemade baby food:

- Small cooking pot or saucepan with lid
- Metal spoon for stirring
- Kitchen weighing scale
- Measuring spoons and cups
- Cutting board, knife, vegetable peeler
- Spoons and forks

- Bowls
- Hand-held blender or food processor
- Sieve
- Ice cube tray
- Plastic re-sealable bags

Organic Food

Organic food is becoming increasingly popular, as it is perceived to be safer, more nutritious and more environmentally-friendly. However, much confusion remains as to what "organic" means and how it relates to our lifestyle.

Essentially, organic food:

- Is environmentally friendly as it promotes sustainable use of soil, water and air, and encourages natural biological diversity.
- Does not contain antibiotics or growth hormones.
- Is not grown using synthetic pesticides or fertilisers.
- Does not include genetically modified crops.

The main difference between organic and conventionally grown food is essentially the way it is grown, farmed and handled, which makes organic produce more expensive. Despite these differences, the nutritional value of organic food is similar to that of conventionally grown foods.

If you are willing to pay the higher price for organic food, remember to:

- Buy from a supermarket or store that provides reassurance on the quality of the produce. Check out the baby food section or the organic food aisles to find suitable foods.
- Look out for organic products certified by authorities. Most of them carry a special stamp of certification.
- As with all foods, read labels thoroughly if you are looking for a healthier choice. Some organic foods may be high in fat, sugar, salt or calories, so choose healthier options.

So, is organic food better for your baby? Not necessarily. While organic foods can reduce your baby's exposure to chemical pesticides and fertilisers, they are no safer or more nutritious than regular food.

Get your baby off to a healthy start with regular food this way:

- Offer your baby a wide variety of healthy foods from the beginning.
- Wash all fruit and vegetables thoroughly with running water to reduce the amount of dirt and bacteria present. Use a small scrub brush to clean hardier produce like potatoes and carrots more thoroughly.

Food Safety Tips

Food safety is a critical issue when it comes to the preparation of baby's food and drinks. Disease-causing germs or their toxins, if found in baby's food, can cause stomach discomfort, nausea, vomiting and diarrhoea. In young infants, food poisoning can be fatal. Here are some tips to preparing safe homemade baby food, as well as using commercial foods. Remember, proper hand washing, preparation and storage can prevent spoilage.

- Wash your hands with soap before cooking or preparing food.
- Buy food from reliable suppliers and store them correctly.
- All utensils, cutlery and equipment used must be washed thoroughly and dried.
- Cook food thoroughly as heat destroys most food poisoning germs and toxins.
- Any extra food prepared must be cooled quickly and stored in clean, dry containers in the refrigerator or freezer.
- Do not leave cooked food at room temperature for more than 1 hour.
- Do not refreeze thawed baby food.
- Discard food leftover in baby's bowl or plate.
- Do not feed baby directly from a storage container or jar if not feeding the entire container. It is always safer to spoon a portion of it into a bowl or plate.
- Ensure that the safety seal on commercial baby food is not broken before using.
- Heating or cooking infant food in the microwave oven can cause dangerous hot spots. If using the microwave oven, stir the heated food evenly and check the temperature of the food or liquid before serving. Baby's food only needs to be at body temperature, not hot.

Safety Issues

- Honey may contain spores that cause botulism. The AAP recommends that honey not be given to infants under 12 months of age because spores of Clostridium botulinum can grow in it and cause a potentially fatal illness in infants.

- Raw eggs may be contaminated with salmonella causing food poisoning. Babies can be given well-cooked egg yolks after nine months of age.

**Foods To Avoid
In The First Year**
- Honey
- Raw eggs
- Raw fish, undercooked meat and raw salads
- Unpasteurised milk
- Foods that may cause choking, such as:
  - whole grapes with skin
  - fishballs
  - nuts and seeds
  - large pieces of food
  - poultry or fish with bones

- Unpasteurised milk or food may contain germs that cause diarrhoea and serious infections.

- Do not add cereal or other solids to milk in baby's bottle. Baby needs to learn to eat solids. Drinking cereal will not allow your child to learn to chew and swallow skilfully. Some babies also swallow a lot of air during this process as they need to suck much harder to drink the cereal-milk mix and this can cause discomfort.

- Be aware of choking risks in infants.
  - Always supervise your baby when feeding.
  - Serve appropriate food for your child's chewing and swallowing abilities.

Are You Ready to Start?

Start out with these easy and delicious recipes. We strongly suggest that you taste them before serving to your child — you will be surprised at how delicious they can be! These recipes do not require any seasoning, nor should you be giving your child any seasoning such as salt, soy sauce or chilli before the age of one. Think of your baby as being a blank canvas, open to all new tastes and textures. By holding off on the seasoning, you can teach your baby to enjoy the natural taste of food. It is a known fact that too much sodium (found in salt and soy sauce) can be difficult for baby's immature kidneys to handle. So hold the salt-shaker for now.

All our recipes are for small amounts of food, but it will be more than your baby can eat. Generally, the extra portions can be frozen and thawed for future meals.

purées

Baby's first solid foods are very smooth mixtures called purées. These smooth, thick pastes are ideally suited to baby's eating abilities as baby makes the first transitions from sucking liquids to swallowing solid food.

Making baby's first food is exciting, but young parents who want to give baby the very best start with all good intentions may be overcome by the difficulty of making nourishing foods in small portions. Preparing baby food takes time and effort, but the results are worth it. Most babies do enjoy the tastes and textures of the purées made for them from fresh and nutritious ingredients.

Maximise the nutrient content of baby food by buying fresh food whenever possible. Wash them well before preparing for cooking. Some fruit are naturally soft and can easily be made into first food purées by blending. Other fruit and vegetables need to be cooked until soft to make them suitable for early introduction.

Steaming is a great way to cook fruit and vegetables for baby, as there is minimal nutritional loss. Boiling can also be used for hardier roots and vegetables, but use only a small amount of water and retain the liquid for use in soups or stews. Using pressure cookers and microwave ovens are also convenient and save time. Whichever cooking method you choose to use, always allow the cooked fruit or vegetables to cool a little before puréeing with a hand-held blender or food processor. Serve the purée when it is still warm.

To maximise your cooking efforts, a larger serving of purée can be prepared, then put into an ice cube tray in the freezer. The frozen cubes of purée can then be removed from the ice cube tray and kept in re-sealable plastic bags marked with the contents and date of preparation. These fruit and vegetable ices can be defrosted and gently warmed up for a quick, nourishing meal for baby when you are rushed for time. Adjust the consistency of the purées, if needed, with small amounts of breast milk or formula.

For older babies who are beginning to experiment with texture, purées can be lumpier and include finely chopped pieces of vegetables or fruit. For example, instead of using a blender or food processor to make apple purée, use a fork or potato masher to mash up the steamed apple pieces.

Iron-fortified Commercial Baby Rice Cereal

Makes 3 tsp

Iron-fortified baby rice cereal is the best first food choice for baby. Rice is the least allergenic grain and is easily handled by your baby's digestive system. Home-cooked rice porridge is also great for this purpose, but only iron-fortified baby rice cereal provides the much-needed iron to restore baby's liver stores at this stage.

Nutrient Analysis
Per 1 tsp serving

Energy 4 kcals
Protein 0 g
Carbohydrates 1 g
Total fat 0 g
Saturated fat 0 g
Cholesterol 0 mg
Dietary fibre 0 g
Sodium 1 mg
Calcium 3 mg
Iron 0.1 mg

For a start...

Iron-fortified baby rice cereal powder *1 tsp*
Breast milk or reconstituted infant formula *2 tsp*

Later on... *Makes a little more than ¹/₂ cup*

Iron-fortified baby rice cereal powder *3 Tbsp (30 g / 1 oz)*
Breast milk or reconstituted infant formula *6 Tbsp (90 ml / 3 fl oz)*

1   Spoon the iron-fortified baby rice cereal into a small feeding bowl.

2   Add the milk and stir well to make it smooth and runny. Serve immediately.

✳ Measure out the right portion into the mixing bowl to prepare just one serving.

✳ If baby is still willing to try more, prepare a fresh new batch.

✳ Any remaining cereal powder must be stored in a clean, dry and airtight container.

Vegetable Purées

Sweet Potato Purée *Makes ³/₄ cup*

Sweet potatoes are an excellent source of vitamins A and C. They are also high in complex carbohydrates, dietary fibre, vitamin B₆ and potassium. The natural sweetness and bright colour makes sweet potatoes an appetising addition to your baby's food adventure!

Nutrient Analysis Per 2 Tbsp serving

Energy 34 kcals
Protein 1 g
Carbohydrates 7 g
Total fat 0 g
Saturated fat 0 g
Cholesterol 1 mg
Dietary fibre 1 g
Sodium 20 mg
Calcium 13 mg
Iron 0.2 mg

Sweet potato *1, about 200 g (7 oz)*

1 Wash, then cut the sweet potato into medium-size pieces.

2 Steam the sweet potato for 10–15 minutes, or until cooked through and tender.

3 Drain and allow the sweet potato to cool slightly. Scoop out the sweet potato flesh from the skin. Discard the skin.

4 Use a hand-held blender or food processor to make a smooth purée. Serve immediately.

TIPS

* Sweet potatoes should be stored in a well-ventilated place away from direct sunlight, and they should not be kept in plastic bags.

* Sweet potatoes should never be eaten raw as they can be toxic.

Pea Purée *Makes ¹/₂ cup*

Green peas may be small in size, but they pack a powerful punch in terms of minerals and vitamins. They are a very good source of protein and fibre, as well as vitamin A, vitamin C, thiamin (vitamin B$_1$), folate, iron and phosphorus.

**Nutrient Analysis
Per 2 Tbsp serving**

Energy 29 kcals
Protein 2 g
Carbohydrates 5 g
Total fat 0 g
Saturated fat 0 g
Cholesterol 0 mg
Dietary fibre 2.1 g
Sodium 27 mg
Calcium 9 mg
Iron 0.6 mg

Fresh or frozen green peas *150 g (5¹/₃ oz / 1 cup)*

1   Steam the green peas for 5 minutes or until tender. If using frozen peas, steam them straight from the freezer. It is not necessary to thaw them first before steaming. Drain and allow the peas to cool.

2   Use a hand-held blender or food processor to make a smooth purée.

3   Press the pea purée through a fine-mesh sieve using the back of a spoon. Discard the pea skins. Serve immediately.

✳ A large proportion of green peas grown are frozen or canned before arriving on the supermarket shelves. Choose frozen peas over canned peas as they are lower in sodium, and are able to retain their colour, flavour and nutrients better.

Pumpkin Purée *Makes ³/₄ cup*

Pumpkins are an abundant source of beta-carotene, the natural yellow-coloured pigment, which the body can turn into vitamin A. Pumpkins are also a good source of complex carbohydrates and dietary fibre. They also contain iron and a fair amount of vitamin C, folate, magnesium and potassium. Pumpkins are sometimes referred to as squash.

**Nutrient Analysis
Per 2 Tbsp serving**

Energy 13 kcals
Protein 0 g
Carbohydrates 3 g
Total fat 0 g
Saturated fat 0 g
Cholesterol 0 mg
Dietary fibre 0.2 g
Sodium 1 mg
Calcium 10 mg
Iron 0.3 mg

Pumpkin or butternut squash *250 g (9 oz)*

1   Scrape out the pumpkin seeds and cut the pumpkin into medium-size pieces.

2   Steam the pumpkin for 10–15 minutes, or until cooked through and tender.

3   Drain and allow the pumpkin to cool slightly. Scoop out the pumpkin flesh from the skin. Discard the skin.

4   Use a hand-held blender or food processor to make a smooth purée. Serve immediately.

＊ When selecting pumpkins, look for firm, round, heavy fruit that are blemish-free. The flesh must also be bright and moist.

＊ A whole pumpkin may be difficult to handle — buy a quarter or half. Cut portions are available in supermarkets and wet markets.

Spinach Purée *Makes $^1/_4$ cup*

In Southeast Asia, the vegetable commonly known as Chinese spinach, *yin choy* or *bayam* is in fact a variety of amaranth that is grown for its tender leaves. While not actually a spinach, the vegetable is commonly labelled as such in supermarkets. You can choose either spinach or Chinese spinach for this recipe. The latter tends to be less bitter in taste.

Both spinach and Chinese spinach are very good sources of vitamins including vitamin A, vitamin B_6, vitamin C, riboflavin (vitamin B_2) and folate. They are also high in minerals like calcium, iron and zinc.

**Nutrient Analysis
Per 2 Tbsp serving**

Energy 4 kcals
Protein 1 g
Carbohydrates 0 g
Total fat 0 g
Saturated fat 0 g
Cholesterol 0 mg
Dietary fibre 2.8 g
Sodium 39 mg
Calcium 26 mg
Iron 2.2 mg

Spinach *1 small bunch, 65 g ($2^1/_3$ oz)*

1   Cut off and discard the spinach roots. Wash the spinach well, then drain.

2   Bring some water to the boil in a pot. Add the spinach and cook for 1–2 minutes. Drain and allow the spinach to cool.

3   Use a hand-held blender or food processor to make a smooth purée. Serve immediately.

TIPS

✳ When choosing spinach, choose those with vibrant green leaves and stems that show no signs of yellowing. The leaves should look fresh and tender, and not be wilted or bruised.

✳ Store the fresh and loosely packed spinach in a plastic bag in the vegetable chiller section of the refrigerator, where it should remain fresh for a few days.

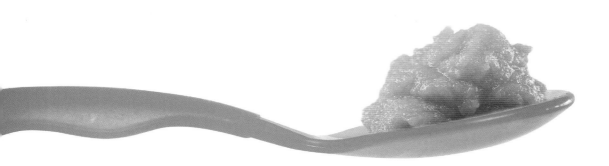

Carrot Purée *Makes 1 cup*

Carrots are also an excellent source of beta-carotene. Vitamin A is essential for maintaining good vision, while carotenoids have anti-oxidant properties. Beta-carotene is not destroyed by cooking; in fact, cooking breaks down the fibre in carrots, making the beta-carotene and natural sugars more available, and gives the carrots a sweeter taste.

Nutrient Analysis
Per 2 Tbsp serving

Energy 12 kcals
Protein 0 g
Carbohydrates 3 g
Total fat 0 g
Saturated fat 0 g
Cholesterol 1 mg
Dietary fibre 0.9 g
Sodium 23 mg
Calcium 12 mg
Iron 0.1 mg

Carrots *5, small, 250 g (9 oz)*

1 Peel and wash the carrots, then cut them into medium-size pieces.

2 Steam the carrots for 10–15 minutes, or until cooked through and tender. Drain and allow the carrots to cool slightly.

3 Use a hand-held blender or food processor to make a smooth purée. Serve immediately.

✳ Choose carrots that are firm, smooth and bright in colour. Large carrots contain more beta-carotene and are also sweeter, so choose them over baby carrots.

✳ Carrots are hardy vegetables that can keep for a couple of weeks, if stored properly in the refrigerator. Preserve their freshness by keeping them in a plastic bag or wrapped in a paper towel. If the green tops are still attached, cut the tops off before storing in the refrigerator to prevent the roots from losing moisture.

✳ Always wash and peel carrots before using.

Fruit Purées

Honeydew or Rock Melon Purée *Makes ³/₄ cup*

Honeydew and rock melons are favourite foods among babies and children due to their juicy and fragrant sweetness. Honeydew has a white or pale green rind and a light green or white flesh. It is high in vitamin C and is a good source of potassium. Rock melon has a green rind and peachy orange flesh. It is also high in vitamin C, and is a good source of vitamin A, vitamin B_6 and folate.

**Nutrient Analysis
Per 2 Tbsp serving**

Energy 26 kcals

Protein 0 g

Carbohydrates 6 g

Total fat 0 g

Saturated fat 0 g

Cholesterol 0 mg

Dietary fibre 0.5 g

Sodium 12 mg

Calcium 9 mg

Iron 0.4 mg

Ripe honeydew or rock melon *400 g (14 ¹/₃ oz)*
Baby rice cereal (optional) *4 tsp*

1 Scrape out and discard the melon seeds. Cut the melon into medium-size pieces, then scoop out the flesh from the skin. Discard the skin.

2 Use a hand-held blender or food processor to make a smooth purée.

3 **If the consistency of the purée is too thin, thicken it with some baby rice cereal. Add the rice cereal 1 tsp at a time until the desired consistency is achieved. Use breast milk or formula to adjust the consistency further, if needed.**

TIPS

* Choose unblemished melons that seem heavy for their size. The area where the stem was attached should be smooth and slightly indented.

* You should also be able to smell the fruit's sweet fragrance from the bottom of the melon. However, do not choose melons with an overly strong aroma, as the fruit may be overripe and fermented.

* If freezing melon purée, freeze only the pure purée, without the added breast milk, formula or baby rice cereal. If refrigerating, cover with plastic wrap (cling film) and discard if not consumed within 24 hours.

Banana Purée *Makes ¹/₂ cup*

Ripe bananas are an excellent food for weaning babies. A popular and staple food in tropical Southeast Asia, they are very easy to digest and can supply the extra energy and vitamins that babies need. Bananas are a good source of vitamin B₆, vitamin C, potassium and fibre. Potassium aids nerve and muscle development.

Nutrient Analysis
Per 2 Tbsp serving

Energy 22 kcals
Protein 0 g
Carbohydrates 6 g
Total fat 0 g
Saturated fat 0 g
Cholesterol 0 mg
Dietary fibre 0.7 g
Sodium 0 mg
Calcium 1 mg
Iron 0.1 mg

Ripe banana *1, large, about 100 g (3¹/₂ oz)*

1 Peel the banana, then cut it into small pieces and place into a small bowl. Mash with a fork until smooth. Make sure there are no lumpy pieces of banana in the purée.

2 Serve immediately.

* Remember to use ripe bananas, as the starch in unripe bananas is not easily digested. Generally, bananas are ripe when brown spots appear on their skins.

* Store and ripen fresh bananas at room temperature and not in the refrigerator.

* Serve banana purée as soon as possible after preparing, as it oxidises quickly.

* Banana purée cannot be frozen for later use.

Apple Purée *Makes ³/₄ cup*

The adage goes, "an apple a day keeps the doctor away" — apples are indeed amazing. The natural pectin in apples aid in regulating baby's bowels, helps constipated babies release softer stools and enables babies suffering from loose motions to form firmer stools. Apples are a good source of niacin, fibre and vitamin C, and can be easily prepared to make delicious applesauce or purée that babies will love.

**Nutrient Analysis
Per 2 Tbsp serving**

Energy 28 kcals

Protein 0 g

Carbohydrates 7 g

Total fat 0 g

Saturated fat 0 g

Cholesterol 0 mg

Dietary fibre 1.3 g

Sodium 1 mg

Calcium 3 mg

Iron 0.1 mg

Red apples *2, small, about 320 g (11¹/₃ oz)*

1 Wash, then core the apples. Cut the apples into quarters, then steam for 15–20 minutes, or until cooked through and tender.

2 Drain and allow the apples to cool. Scoop out the apple flesh from the skin. Discard the skin.

3 Use a hand-held blender or food processor to make a smooth purée. Serve immediately.

TIPS

✳ Select sweet red apples to make baby's first foods. Tart fruit may make baby reject apples.

✳ Steam the apples with the skin on, then scrape off the flesh to maximise nutrient retention.

Pear Purée *Makes 1 cup*

Pears have a fragrant and subtle sweetness that baby will find hard to resist! Pears are a good source of vitamin C, folate and dietary fibre, and are one of the fruit least likely to produce an adverse reaction in babies. Pear purée is a particularly tasty first food.

Nutrient Analysis Per 2 Tbsp serving

Energy 22 kcals
Protein 0 g
Carbohydrates 6 g
Total fat 0 g
Saturated fat 0 g
Cholesterol 0 mg
Dietary fibre 1.2 g
Sodium 0 mg
Calcium 3 mg
Iron 0.1 mg

Ripe pears (Bartlett, D'Anjou or Bosc) *2, small, about 300 g (11 oz)*

1 Wash, then core the pears. Cut them into quarters, then steam for 15–20 minutes, or until cooked through and tender.

2 Drain and allow the pears to cool. Scoop out the pear flesh from the skin. Discard the skin.

3 Use a hand-held blender or food processor to make a smooth purée. Serve immediately.

 TIPS

✳ Pears found in supermarkets or markets are often unripe. Set them aside at room temperature for a couple of days to ripen. They are ready for use when they yield to gentle pressure.

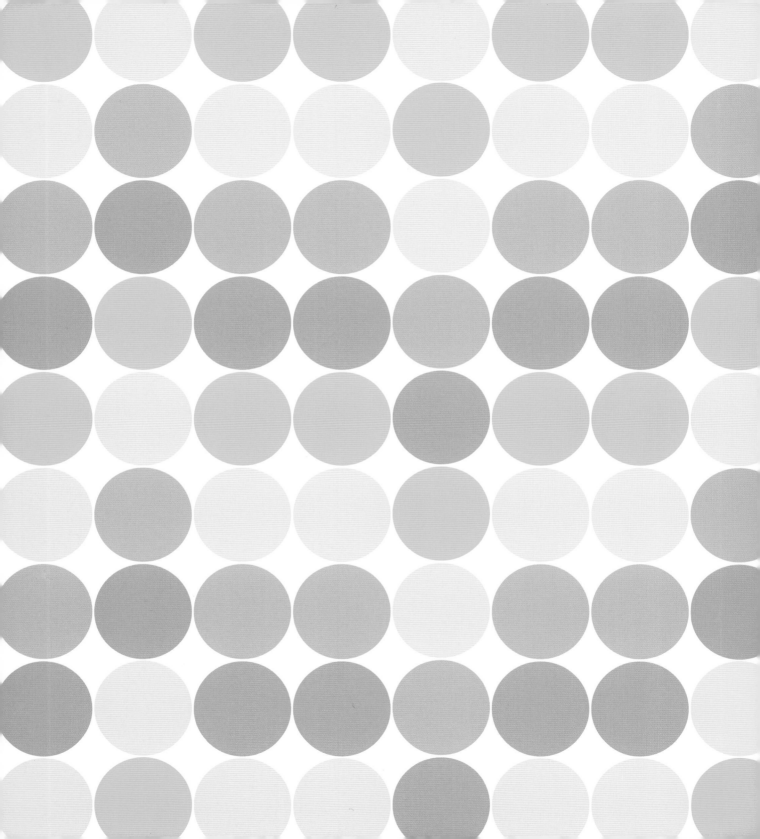

savouring more flavours and textures

6 to 9 months of age

Introduce a Wider Range of New Foods

As soon as you think you have mastered the art of purées, your baby will be ready to experiment with new textures and new tastes, in addition to the usual milk feeds! Although it is not time to put away the blender yet, you will want to make the texture of the final product a little lumpier than a purée, so your baby will gradually become used to the change and be more accepting of new textures.

This texture transition is important to gently guide your little one toward eating family foods after the age of one year. Do not panic if your baby refuses or spits out the lumpier food, and do not revert to offering just smooth purées. Stay the course and you will soon be surprised how quickly your baby picks up new chewing and swallowing skills.

Once your baby has tried and tasted single ingredients and then, combinations of foods, you can confidently add new flavours. Between the ages of six and nine months, we recommend recipes incorporating new fruit flavours such as papaya, peach and apricot; vegetables like avocado, broccoli and potato, as well as moving into single protein foods like chicken, fish and lentils. This section also includes basic recipes like stocks and plain porridge to be used with a variety of other ingredients.

While it may be convenient to serve up all the nutritious foods in one bowl or as part of one recipe, do not make this a common practice. Serve foods separately to allow your baby to recognise and appreciate new foods.

Ensure Food Safety

Although your baby is now a little older, food safety continues to be crucial. It is of particular concern when preparing protein food, like meat, as there is a higher risk for contamination. Always wash your hands before food preparation and before serving meals to your baby. Cross-contamination occurs when micro-organisms, like bacteria, are transferred from one place, or food, to another. One of the most common examples is when the same cutting board is used for cutting raw meat and vegetables. To avoid the risk of cross-contamination, use a dedicated cutting board for preparing raw meats and another for vegetables. Additionally, always ensure that meat items are well-cooked to avoid the chances of contracting any food-borne illness. Meat is cooked when it is no longer pink inside.

Keep Milk Feeds Going

You will find that your baby is now drinking larger amounts of milk per feed but, as he consumes more solid food, you can cut back the milk portion at the scheduled meal time to allow him to enjoy a larger portion of solid food. Nutritionally, however, milk remains the most important component of a baby's diet.

If you want to add milk, other than breast milk, to your baby's diet, do not use cow's milk. The reason cow's milk is restricted before baby turns one, is because the protein in the milk can be difficult for young, immature digestive systems to handle. Your baby's kidneys also cannot manage the nutrient composition of cow's milk until they are more developed.

Dairy foods that are made from cow's milk, such as mild cheese and yoghurt, however, can be introduced in small amounts before 12 months. This is because their nutritional composition is slightly different from cow's milk, and can be managed by your baby's digestive system. If a recipe calls for milk at this stage, use breast milk or suitably prepared infant formula.

Going Vegetarian

Vegetarianism is a way of eating that generally includes all plant or plant-based foods and excludes most meat, poultry and fish or other animal-based foods, such as gelatine or lard.

There are many different variations of the vegetarian way of eating; some exclude milk, while others exclude all types of animal-based food.

Regardless of your reason for being vegetarian or your choice for your baby to become vegetarian, it is important to provide your baby with adequate energy, protein, vitamins and minerals to meet baby's nutritional needs. The stage of the most rapid growth in a child's life is typically between six and 18 months, so any restriction in diet can be a cause for concern. A varied and well thought out vegetarian diet for your baby, however, can be healthy and provide adequate nutrients.

The key to a healthy vegetarian diet is to include complementary plant proteins that will provide good quality alternative protein sources to animal-based foods. Because many plant proteins do not contain sufficient essential amino acids, they are considered incomplete proteins. To meet our daily nutrient requirement of proteins, it is necessary to consume complementary plant proteins, or pair two plant proteins, so the amino acids lacking in one plant protein can be supplied by the other, to create a more complete protein.

"I am not a vegetarian because I love animals; I am a vegetarian because I hate plants."

A. Whitney Brown

Examples of complementary proteins include:

- Tofu and rice
- Beans and tortillas or chapati
- Chickpeas and rice
- Rice and dhal
- Dhosai and mild sambar (lentil curry)

The major nutrients of concern based on type of vegetarianism, are as follows:

- Lacto (includes milk) or lacto-ovo (includes milk and eggs): Iron
- Vegan (no milk or eggs): Vitamin B_{12}, vitamin D, iron

If you are vegetarian and plan on feeding your baby as one, but are unsure how to proceed, speak to your baby's paediatrician or GP and a dietitian to ensure that you are feeding suitable and appropriate foods that will meet your baby's needs.

Increase Serving Sizes

By now, you will find that your baby is gradually taking more solid food, up from the initial one to two teaspoons to about one-quarter or half cup. You will also find that you are getting better at reading your baby's signals. But, many parents are still unsure of how to feed their baby. This is normal, as your baby will be hungrier on some days than others, although it can be a source of frustration to many well-meaning parents.

Closing his eyes, turning his head away or clamping his mouth shut may be signs that your baby is full. This is where you need to trust your baby and respect his wishes. Force-feeding your baby because you were taught to clean your plate when young, usually results in disaster and may teach your baby not to listen to his own internal hunger and satiety cues.

Serving sizes are difficult to map out since each baby is different and as a result have different needs. The best way to start is to make a small amount of food and offer seconds (and thirds!) if your baby seems interested in more. Weighing in at regular developmental checks and plotting your baby's growth along the growth curve will help you know if you are feeding your baby enough or too much. A healthy baby's weight will plot parallel to a set growth curve. Rapid weight gain or weight loss can alert you to adjust portions. If you are unsure, consult your baby's paediatrician, GP or a dietitian to help you make sense of your baby's weight records.

Food Additive Worries

Food additives include a range of things like minerals or vitamins used to fortify food, preservatives that slow spoilage of certain food, and other substances to enhance the colour, appearance or flavour of food, among others. In most cases, additives are used in the smallest amount needed to achieve the desired effect and are unlikely to cause any reactions. While a very small number of individuals are sensitive to certain additives, there is little evidence to support the view that behaviour and physical or mental development is negatively affected by these compounds. There are some people, however, who are unusually sensitive and may need to avoid certain additives contained in food or medications. Talk to a dietitian if you have any concerns about food additives and your child.

Seafood Safety

Although fish is an important part of a healthy diet since they provide protein and other nutrients, there are some types of seafood, specifically, shellfish like prawns and crab, which we suggest to restrict until your baby is older because of the risk of allergies. This is of more concern if there is a history of food allergies in your family.

Toxins, like heavy metals, are found in very small amounts in shellfish, so the concern lies primarily with larger fish. The heavy metal, mercury, is found naturally in the environment but gets concentrated in bodies of water, primarily through industrial pollution, and is eventually absorbed by fish in the water. The larger the fish, the higher the concentration, so regulatory agencies, like the United States Food and Drug Administration (US FDA), advise limiting consumption of shark, swordfish, king mackerel and tilefish. People most at risk are babies under 12 months old, pregnant and lactating women, and even women trying to conceive. This may sound alarming, but while we need to be cautious, we must also remember that seafood, as well as fish, provide important nutrients like protein, omega-3 and omega-6 fatty acids which are important for brain development. As dietitians, we recommend fish and seafood intake for your growing child as the health benefits outweigh the risk of heavy metal exposure. From a food allergy perspective, however, it is best to wait until after age one before introducing shellfish, especially if food allergies run in the family.

MASHED WITH SOFT PIECES

INGREDIENTS: PUMPKIN (36%),
WHEAT COUSCOUS (21%), POTATOES,
WATER, GREEN PEAS, CARROTS,
UNSALTED BUTTER, TAPIOCA FLOUR,
ZUCCHINI, SPINACH, NATURAL ONION
FLAVOUR, SPICE EXTRACT.

NUTRITION INFORMATION

SERVINGS PER PACKAGE: 1		
SERVING SIZE: 170g	AVERAGE QUANTITY	
	PER SERVING	PER 100g
ENERGY	390kJ	230kJ
PROTEIN	2.5g	1.5g
FAT, TOTAL	2.2g	1.3g
CARBOHYDRATE	14.1g	8.3g
- SUGARS	4.3g	2.5g
DIETARY FIBRE	2.9g	1.7g
SODIUM	12mg	7mg
POTASSIUM	340mg	200mg

more purées and porridges

Now that your baby is familiar with eating and swallowing, and has a familiar repertoire of cereals, fruit and vegetables, you are ready to introduce more flavours and combinations.

The recipes in this section include more fruit and vegetable choices, and introduce delicious food combinations for baby. You will also find many basic recipes for stocks and porridges, which you can use to create new recipes for your growing baby.

We will also start to introduce other protein-rich foods, such as fish, chicken and pork, as well as vegetarian-friendly bean and soy-based recipes, to ensure your baby receives enough protein each day.

These recipes will continue to focus on offering your baby a variety of single foods or simple combinations to allow baby to appreciate new flavours and delicious combinations. In using these recipes, do bear in mind to avoid making up the same combinations every day, even though baby seems to love it. After some time, your little one will be bored with the combination and will begin to fuss.

More Single Fruit Purées

Peach Purée *Makes ¹/₂ cup*

Peaches are sweet and juicy when ripe and they make a lip-smacking purée that baby will love. Peaches come in a range of colours — white, yellow or pink — with tones of orange and red. Bright-coloured peaches are high in the immunity-boosters, beta-carotene, vitamin C and vitamin E. In Chinese tradition, it is regarded as symbol of longevity and good health.

Nutrient Analysis Per 3 Tbsp serving

Energy 19 kcals
Protein 0 g
Carbohydrates 5 g
Total fat 0 g
Saturated fat 0 g
Cholesterol 0 mg
Dietary fibre 0.8 g
Sodium 0 mg
Calcium 3 mg
Iron 0.1 mg

Fresh, ripe peach *1, about 130 g (4¹/₂ oz)*

or

Peach halves, canned in juice *2, about 196 g (7 oz)*

1 If using fresh peaches, wash and peel the fruit, then cut into quarters and remove the pits. Steam the peaches for 10 minutes or until soft. Allow the peaches to cool before making the purée.

2 If using canned peaches, skip the step above. Simply drain the peach halves and purée the fruit.

3 Use a hand-held blender or food processor to make a smooth purée. Serve immediately.

TIPS

* Peaches can be messy to peel. A good way of minimising the mess is to cut a small cross at the tip of the fruit, then blanch it in hot water for 1 minute. Remove the peach from the hot water, then rinse it in cold water. Peel the skin starting from the tip.

* Avoid using peaches canned in light or heavy syrup. The added sugar is not something that your baby needs at this stage and it will also take away the natural sweetness of the fruit.

Avocado Purée *Makes ¹/₂ cup*

Avocados are loved for their creamy, buttery texture. High in nutrients such as fibre, potassium, vitamin E, B vitamins and folate, avocados also contain beneficial unsaturated fats.

**Nutrient Analysis
Per 3 Tbsp serving**

Energy 130 kcals
Protein 2 g
Carbohydrates 6 g
Total fat 11 g
Saturated fat 1.8 g
Cholesterol 0 mg
Dietary fibre 3.8 g
Sodium 8 mg
Calcium 8 mg
Iron 0.8 mg

Ripe avocado *1 small, about 200 g (7 oz)*

1 Cut the avocado in half lengthwise, then remove the stone by sliding the tip of a spoon beneath it and lifting the stone out.

2 If the avocado is sufficiently ripe, you should be able to scoop out the flesh using a spoon. If not, slide a knife between the peel and flesh to separate the two. Scoop out the avocado flesh.

3 If the avocado is soft enough, mash well using the back of a fork. Alternatively, use a hand-held blender or food processor to make a smooth purée. Serve immediately.

TIPS

* The best way to tell if an avocado is ripe and ready-to-eat, is to gently squeeze the fruit in the palm of your hand. It should be firm yet yield to gentle pressure. Avoid avocados that are overly soft or bruised.

* If the avocado is unripe, set it aside at room temperature and it should ripen in 2 to 5 days.

* The Hass avocado, which is found in most supermarkets, turns dark green or black as it ripens.

Variation

For older toddlers, cut the avocado flesh into wedges to be eaten as finger food.

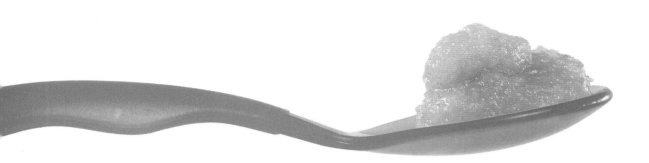

Apricot Purée *Makes ¹/₂ cup*

Apricots are a very good source of vitamins A (beta-carotene) and C. They also contribute potassium, iron, calcium, phosphorus and fibre to baby's diet. As apricots are a seasonal fruit, you may not be able to find them in the supermarkets or markets all-year round. Dried apricots, however, are easily available and can also be used to make a sweet treat for baby.

Nutrient Analysis
Per 3 Tbsp serving

Energy 13 kcals
Protein 1 g
Carbohydrates 3 g
Total fat 0 g
Saturated fat 0 g
Cholesterol 0 mg
Dietary fibre 0.5 g
Sodium 1 mg
Calcium 4 mg
Iron 0.1 mg

Fresh, ripe apricots *2, about 70 g (2¹/₂ oz)*
or
Dried pitted apricots *18, about 80 g (2²/₃ oz)*

1 If using fresh apricots, wash, then peel the fruit. Cut into quarters and remove pit. Steam the apricots for 10 minutes or until tender.

2 If using dried apricots, wash the fruit thoroughly. Steam or gently simmer for 20–30 minutes or until soft. If simmering, stir frequently so the apricots do not burn or stick to the pan.

3 Drain and allow the cooked apricots to cool.

4 Mash the cooked apricots using the back of a fork, or use a hand-held blender or food processor to make a smooth purée. Serve immediately.

＊ Select fresh apricots that are round, firm, blemish-free and heavy for their size.

＊ Pick unsweetened, sulfur-free dried apricots for baby's meal.

Papaya Purée *Makes ½ cup*

The papaya is a wonderful tropical fruit that can be enjoyed all-year round. With its bright orange flesh, the fruit is a rich source of anti-oxidant nutrients such as beta-carotene and vitamin C. High in fibre, papaya is also a good source of vitamin E, B vitamins and folate. Papaya is one of the most nutritious tropical fruit. Choose papayas that are ripe, but not overly soft.

Nutrient Analysis
Per 3 Tbsp serving

Energy 28 kcals
Protein 0 g
Carbohydrates 7 g
Total fat 0 g
Saturated fat 0 g
Cholesterol 0 mg
Dietary fibre 1.3 g
Sodium 2 mg
Calcium 17 mg
Iron 0.1 mg

Ripe papaya *1, small, about 190 g (6²/₃ oz)*

1   Wash the papaya, then cut in half lengthwise. Scoop out the papaya seeds and discard. Scoop out the flesh and discard the skin.

2   Use the back of a fork to mash the papaya, or a hand-held blender to make a smooth purée. Serve immediately.

Delicious Blends

Homemade Yoghurt and Fruit Purée

Makes about $^3/_4$ cup

Yoghurt is made by fermenting milk with bacterial cultures. The fermentation of milk sugar (lactose) produces lactic acid, which gels the milk protein to give yoghurt its unique texture and tang. Yoghurt is gentler on the stomach than milk, and is a good source of protein and calcium.

If you are unfamiliar with yoghurt, you may be surprised by the sour taste. Many commercial yoghurt products use a lot of sugar to mask the tart flavour. It is best to introduce a very mild yoghurt to baby, and homemade yoghurt is a good option. By controlling the time allowed for the yoghurt to set, you can minimise its sourness, and you do not need to add sugar. If you are worried about food safety, rest assured that the natural acidity of yoghurt prevents the growth of harmful bacteria. It really is simple to make natural yoghurt at home. Give it a try and you will probably also enjoy this delicious recipe!

**Nutrient Analysis
Per 3 Tbsp serving**

Energy 20 kcals
Protein 0 g
Carbohydrates 5 g
Total fat 0 g
Saturated fat 0 g
Cholesterol 2 mg
Dietary fibre 0.8 g
Sodium 5 mg
Calcium 16 mg
Iron 0.1 mg

Fresh whole pasteurised milk *125 ml (4 fl oz / $^1/_2$ cup)*
Natural yoghurt *$^1/_4$ tsp*
Apple purée or other naturally sweet fruit purée *4 Tbsp*

1   Warm the milk in a saucepan over low heat, until about body temperature. Pour the milk into a bowl, then add the natural yoghurt and stir well.

2   Cover the bowl with a lid or plastic wrap (cling film) and leave it at room temperature to set for no more than 12 hours.

3   Spoon the set yoghurt into a bowl, add fruit purée and mix well.

TIPS

✳ Homemade yoghurt can be stored in the refrigerator for up to 3 days.

✳ Ask your Indian neighbours or an Indian restaurant for a teaspoon of natural yoghurt to set your first batch of yoghurt. Plain yoghurt with live cultures available in the supermarket can also be used.

✳ The longer you leave the yoghurt at room temperature, the tangier the yoghurt becomes.

✳ Any remaining yoghurt left in the refrigerator can provide the starter culture for your next batch of yoghurt.

Variation

Experiment with different fruit options to create tasty treats for your little one. Here are a few ideas:

- Mashed or chopped banana
- Puréed or finely chopped mango
- Mashed or chopped papaya

Carrot and Potato Purée *Makes about ³/₄ cup*

The combined sweetness of carrots and the creamy texture of mashed potato makes this an all-time favourite.

Nutrient Analysis Per 3 Tbsp serving

Energy 41 kcals
Protein 1 g
Carbohydrates 9 g
Total fat 0 g
Saturated fat 0 g
Cholesterol 0 mg
Dietary fibre 1.1 g
Sodium 16 mg
Calcium 10 mg
Iron 0.4 mg

Potato *1, small, about 170 g (6 oz)*
Carrot *1, small, about 70 g (2¹/₂ oz)*
Water *250 ml (8 fl oz / 1 cup)*

1 Wash and peel the potato and carrot, then cut into medium-size pieces.

2 Place the carrot and potato pieces in a saucepan and add enough water to cover the vegetables.

3 Simmer the vegetables for 15–20 minutes or until cooked through and tender. Drain and allow the potato and carrot to cool.

4 Use a hand-held blender or food processor to make a smooth purée or use the back of a fork or a potato masher to make a lumpier purée. Serve immediately.

Variation

Try these other yummy combinations:

- Apple and pear
- Pea and pumpkin

Protein-Rich Purées

These purées can be served to baby alone or in combination with vegetable or fruit purées, or with a variety of grain porridges.

Finely Flaked Fish *Makes ³/₄ cup*

Fresh white fish (cod, threadfin *(ikan kurau)*) *150 g (5¹/₃ oz)*
Young ginger *2 thin slices*

1 Clean the fish. Place the ginger slices on the fish and steam for 10 minutes or until the fish is cooked through. Remove and discard ginger.

2 Allow the fish to cool a little before finely flaking the meat using a fork. Be careful to remove any bones.

TIPS

﹡ Select fish with few bones.

﹡ Ask the fishmonger to debone the fish and slice it for you into smaller portions. You can then pack and freeze the fish in small portions and use them as needed.

Pork Purée *Makes ¹/₂ cup*

Nutrient Analysis Per 2 Tbsp serving

Energy 57 kcals
Protein 9 g
Carbohydrates 0 g
Total fat 2 g
Saturated fat 0.8 g
Cholesterol 24 mg
Dietary fibre 0 g
Sodium 22 mg
Calcium 8 mg
Iron 0.3 mg

Homemade chicken/pork stock (see pages **82–83**) or water *250 ml (8 fl oz / I cup)*
Minced pork *I60 g (5²/₃ oz)*

1   Place the homemade chicken/pork stock or water in a small pot or saucepan, and bring to the boil. Add the minced pork and simmer for 3–5 minutes, or until meat is cooked through.

2   Drain, reserving 3 Tbsp of the stock. Allow the pork to cool.

3   Add the reserved stock to the cooled minced pork. Use a food processor or hand-held blender to make a smooth purée. Serve immediately.

✳   Minced pork purées easily. As your baby grows, skip the blending and offer finely minced meat.

✳   Strip loin and loin cuts are tender, and are better cuts to make a softer, smoother purée.

✳   Cook meat thoroughly, but do not overcook, as the meat will become tough.

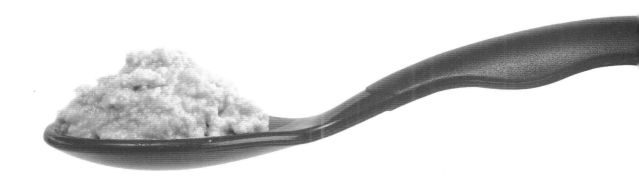

Chicken Purée *Makes ¹/₂ cup*

Homemade chicken stock (see page 82) or water *250 ml (8 fl oz / 1 cup)*
Boneless chicken meat or chicken mince *160 g (5²/₃ oz)*

1   Place the chicken stock or water in a small pot or saucepan and bring to the boil. Add the chicken and simmer over low heat for 5–10 minutes, or until chicken is cooked through.

2   Drain, reserving 3 Tbsp of the stock. Allow the chicken to cool before cutting into small pieces.

3   Add the reserved stock to the chicken. Use a hand-held blender or food processor to make a smooth purée. Serve immediately.

* You can gently simmer the chicken breast in stock, covered or foil wrapped, to make a more tender meat purée.

* Boiled or poached chicken thigh or chicken mince make softer purées than chicken breast.

* Cook poultry thoroughly. Well-cooked meat loses the pink colour in the centre and turns white.

Silken Tofu Mash *Makes ³/₄ cup*

**Nutrient Analysis
Per 2 Tbsp serving**

Energy 15 kcals
Protein 2 g
Carbohydrates 0 g
Total fat 1 g
Saturated fat 0.1 g
Cholesterol 0 mg
Dietary fibre 0.1 g
Sodium 2 mg
Calcium 28 mg
Iron 0.3 mg

Silken tofu *¹/₂ block, 150 g (5¹/₃ oz)*

1   Steam the tofu for 5–10 minutes. Drain the tofu, then allow it to cool a little.

2   Mash the tofu using the back of a fork. Serve immediately.

 TIPS

❋   To make the tofu more flavourful, steam it with vegetable stock (see page 84) or mushrooms.

Homemade Stocks

These stocks will add flavour to your baby's meals. Use them in place of water for porridges, or when making meat purées. We have deliberately created these recipes to produce larger quantities of stock, so they can be frozen for later use. Portion out the stock into smaller containers or into ice cube trays to freeze. You will need to defrost only one small portion to prepare baby's meal. Use the frozen stock within 2 months of freezing.

Chicken Stock *Makes about 1.5 litres (48 fl oz / 6 cups)*

Dried Chinese mushrooms *5*
Water *2 litres (64 fl oz / 8 cups)*
Chicken *800 g (1 ¹/₄ lb), cut into pieces*

1 Wash the dried mushrooms and place them into a small bowl. Add some warm water and leave the mushrooms to soak for about 10 minutes. Drain and set aside.

2 Pour the 2 litres of water into a pot and bring it to the boil. Add the chicken and mushrooms, then cover with a lid.

3 Once the water returns to the boil, reduce heat and gently simmer for 2 hours.

4 When the stock is ready, remove the chicken and mushrooms and strain the stock through a sieve. Allow to cool before using.

* Make a low-fat stock by removing the chicken skin and trimming away the fat from the chicken before making the stock.

Pork Stock *Makes about 1.5 litres (48 fl oz / 6 cups)*

Long Chinese cabbage *500 g (1 lb 1¹/₂ oz)*
Water *2 litres (64 fl oz / 8 cups)*
Pork bones for soup *500 g (1 lb 1¹/₂ oz)*
Spring onions (scallions) *2*

1 Cut the cabbage into medium-size pieces and rinse well.

2 Bring the water to the boil in a pot and add the pork bones. When the water returns to the boil, remove the pot from heat and strain the stock into another pot.

3 Return the pork bones to the strained stock. Add the cabbage and spring onions, then cover the pot with a lid and bring to the boil. When the stock starts to boil, reduce heat and simmer gently for 2 hours.

4 Strain the stock again and allow to cool before using.

 * Select pork bones with some meat for more a flavourful stock.

 * You can use this homemade stock for family meals as well. Use it to flavour stir-fries, moisten noodles and prepare delectable sauces.

Fish Stock *Makes about 1.75 litres (56 fl oz / 7 cups)*

Dried anchovies *(ikan bilis) 200 g (7 oz)*
Water *2 litres (64 fl oz / 8 cups)*

1 Wash the anchovies thoroughly, then drain and set aside.

2 Bring the water to the boil in a pot. Add the anchovies, lower heat and cover the pot with a lid. Simmer for 30 minutes.

3 Strain the stock and allow it to cool before using.

 * Dried anchovies are very high in sodium. Take care to wash them well to reduce the sodium content and to remove any particles of dirt.

 * Alternatively, prepare the fish stock with fish bones or fish meat. This will reduce the sodium content of the stock, particularly when preparing meals for babies younger than 12 months.

Vegetable Stock *Makes about 1.5 litres (48 fl oz / 6 cups)*

White onions *2, medium, about 250 g (9 oz)*
Carrots *2, medium, about 250 g (9 oz)*
Sweet corn *1 ear, about 250 g (9 oz)*
Celery *4 stalks, 250 g (9 oz)*
Long Chinese cabbage *500 g (1 lb 1½ oz)*
Water *2 litres (64 fl oz / 8 cups)*

1   Wash all the vegetables. Peel the onions and carrots. Remove the husk and silk from the sweet corn. Cut all the vegetables into medium-size pieces.

2   Bring the water to the boil in a pot. Add all the chopped vegetables and cover the pot with a lid. When the water returns to boil, lower heat and gently simmer for 2 hours.

3   Strain the stock and allow it to cool before using.

∗   You can also add soy beans, mushrooms and tomatoes to the stock as they have natural flavours that will enhance vegetable stocks.

Porridge

Rice porridge is widely prepared as food for babies in Asia. This one-dish meal is indeed an important foundation food. To further enhance this simple dish, you can vary the grains. Try oats, ragi, infant wheat cereals, semolina and couscous instead of rice. You can also change the vegetable assortment and vary the protein choices. Try beans, lentils, fish and chicken.

Some Practical Tips

- For babies just starting on solids, use a hand-held blender or food processor to grind the uncooked cereal grains to a fine consistency. This will produce a creamy and smooth porridge, and reduce cooking time.

- For babies nine months or older, gradually reduce the grinding of the grains so that baby can experience varying textures. Grinding is not necessary when baby is 12 months or older, and is ready for coarser textures.

- The texture of cooked porridge can also be adjusted to suit baby's development by varying cooking times.

- If using a rice cooker to prepare the porridge, follow the manufacturer's instructions for the amount of water required and the cooking time.

- Porridge is best served freshly prepared. Extra porridge can be kept in the refrigerator for one to two days at the most.

Banana Ragi Porridge *Makes 1 cup*

Ragi, also known as finger millet, is an excellent source of iron and calcium. It is also rich in methionine, an amino acid lacking in most cereals. Ragi has a long tradition of use by Indian mothers as a first food for their babies. In fact, some Indian mothers sprout ragi overnight, then clean and grind the grain to a powder to prepare ragi porridge. Sprouting makes the ragi flour more digestible.

Nutrient Analysis Per $^1/_4$ cup serving

Energy 30 kcals
Protein 1 g
Carbohydrates 7 g
Total fat 0 g
Saturated fat 0 g
Cholesterol 0 mg
Dietary fibre 0.8 g
Sodium 1 mg
Calcium 2 mg
Iron 0.2 mg

Water *170 ml (5$^1/_2$ fl oz / $^2/_3$ cup)*
Ragi flour *20 g ($^2/_3$ oz / 2 Tbsp)*
Ripe banana *$^1/_2$, about 50 g (1$^3/_4$ oz)*

1   Bring the water to the boil in a saucepan. Add the ragi flour, then reduce heat to low.

2   Simmer gently for 5–10 minutes, stirring continuously to achieve a smooth consistency. The porridge is ready when it is smooth and thick. Allow the porridge to cool a little before serving.

3   When porridge is ready for serving, peel the banana, then place it into a small bowl. Mash with the back of a fork, then serve with the porridge.

✳ Ragi flour can be found in most specialty Indian or Asian grocery stores.

✳ Add breast milk or formula to the porridge to achieve a smoother consistency.

Plain Rice Porridge *Makes 3 cups*

**Nutrient Analysis
Per ¼ cup serving**

Energy 31 kcals
Protein 1 g
Carbohydrates 6 g
Total fat 0 g
Saturated fat 0 g
Cholesterol 0 mg
Dietary fibre 0.3 g
Sodium 2 mg
Calcium 4 mg
Iron 0.1 mg

White rice *100 g (3½ oz / ½ cup)*
Homemade stock (see pages 82–84) or water *1 litre (32 fl oz / 4 cups)*

1   Wash the rice and drain.

2   Bring the stock or water to the boil in a pot. Add the rice, lower heat and gently simmer for about 30 minutes, stirring frequently to prevent the porridge from burning or sticking to the pot. The porridge is ready when the consistency is very soft and smooth.

3   Allow the porridge to cool until it is just warm before serving.

* Grinding the rice grains before cooking the porridge will reduce the cooking time and produce a smoother porridge.

* Using homemade stock to prepare the plain porridge will enhance its flavour.

* Compared to white rice, brown rice is higher in fibre and many B vitamins. Prepare a brown rice porridge (*zhao mi /chor bee*) by using brown rice in place of white rice.

Chicken Porridge *Makes ½ cup*

**Nutrient Analysis
Per ¼ cup serving**

Energy 55 kcals
Protein 5 g
Carbohydrates 6 g
Total fat 1 g
Saturated fat 0.2 g
Cholesterol 14 mg
Dietary fibre 0.3 g
Sodium 19 mg
Calcium 7 mg
Iron 0.3 mg

Plain rice porridge (see recipe above) *½ cup*
Chicken purée (see page 80) *2 Tbsp*

1   Prepare the plain rice porridge and the chicken purée.

2   About 5 minutes before the porridge is ready, add the chicken purée and stir well to combine. Allow the porridge to cool until it is just warm before serving.

Variation

This recipe can also be prepared with pork purée or finely flaked fish instead of chicken.

From front to back: Plain Rice Porridge; Plain Brown Rice Porridge

Lentil Porridge *Makes 3 cups*

Lentils are also known as seeds of plants from the legume family. There are a variety of legumes, and their colour ranges from cream to yellow, orange and brown. Green gram or green beans are popular lentils, and they are an excellent source of protein and dietary fibre. They are also high in many minerals including calcium, magnesium and potassium. Lentils are thus an excellent food for babies who are introduced to a vegetarian diet. Lentils can be found in supermarkets and Asian grocers or specialty stores.

Nutrient Analysis Per $^1/_4$ cup serving

Energy 28 kcals
Protein 1 g
Carbohydrates 6 g
Total fat 0 g
Saturated fat 0 g
Cholesterol 0 mg
Dietary fibre 0.2 g
Sodium 3 mg
Calcium 7 mg
Iron 0.4 mg

White rice *50 g (1 $^3/_4$ oz / $^1/_4$ cup)*
Lentils *50 g (1 $^3/_4$ oz / $^1/_4$ cup)*
Homemade vegetable stock (see page 84) *1 litre (32 fl oz / 4 cups)*

1   Wash and drain the rice and lentils. Use a hand-held blender or food processor to grind the rice and lentils until they become a fine powder.

2   Bring the vegetable stock to the boil in a pot. Add the rice and lentil powder and cook for 30 minutes, stirring frequently. The porridge is ready when it is thick and smooth.

3   Allow the porridge to cool until it is just warm before serving.

* Grind extra rice and lentil powder and store it in a clean, dry container in the refrigerator for up to 2 weeks.

Semolina Surprise *Makes 1 cup*

Semolina is broken wheat. It is used to prepare well-known Western staples such as pasta and couscous. This recipe calls for the use of a very fine semolina, commonly used in Indian cooking.

**Nutrient Analysis
Per ¼ cup serving**

Energy 45 kcals

Protein 1 g

Carbohydrates 8 g

Total fat 1 g

Saturated fat 0.3 g

Cholesterol 1 mg

Dietary fibre 0.7 g

Sodium 6 mg

Calcium 6 mg

Iron 0.5 mg

Butter *½ tsp*

Finely grated carrot *1 Tbsp*

Finely minced French beans *1 Tbsp*

Water *3 Tbsp*

Semolina *4 Tbsp*

Homemade vegetable stock (see page 84) *250 ml (8 fl oz / 1 cup)*

1 Heat a small pan over low heat. Melt the butter and do not allow it to burn.

2 Add the grated carrot, minced French beans and water. Cook for 10 minutes or until the vegetables are soft.

3 Add the semolina and stir to mix well. Cook for about 1 minute.

4 Add the vegetable stock and stir quickly to combine so that the semolina is well-hydrated and has a smooth texture. When the semolina is ready, allow it to cool slightly before serving.

✻ Ensure that all the ingredients are cut and cooked to suit your baby's chewing ability.

✻ Semolina is available at Indian or Asian specialty stores.

✻ Vary the vegetables to create new versions of this dish. Try grated potato, finely chopped spinach, cauliflower or finely chopped, ripe and deseeded tomatoes.

Fish and Spinach Porridge *Makes 3 cups*

Nutrient Analysis Per ¹/₂ cup serving

Energy 60 kcals
Protein 3 g
Carbohydrates 12 g
Total fat 0 g
Saturated fat 0 g
Cholesterol 5 mg
Dietary fibre 0.3 g
Sodium 13 mg
Calcium 14 mg
Iron 0.8 mg

White rice *100 g (3¹/₂ oz / 1¹/₂ cup)*
Homemade stock (see pages 82–84) or water *1 litre (32 fl oz / 4 cups)*
Fresh white fish *75 g (2¹/₂ oz)*
Chinese spinach leaves *20 g (²/₃ oz)*

1   Wash the rice and drain.

2   Bring the stock or water to the boil in a pot. Add the rice, lower heat and gently simmer for about 30 minutes, stirring frequently to prevent the porridge from burning or sticking to the pot.

3   Remove all bones from the fish and slice it into small pieces.

4   Wash and drain the Chinese spinach leaves, then chop into small pieces.

5   About 5 minutes before the porridge is ready, add the fish and spinach. Stir to mix well. When the fish and spinach are cooked, remove the porridge from heat and allow the porridge to cool slightly before serving.

 ✳ Shredded carrot or small cubes of pumpkin can be used to replace spinach for a more colourful dish.

expanding baby's food horizons

9 to 12 months of age

This is when things start to get really exciting. Your baby should now be starting to try soft and finely chopped foods, as well as a variety of new flavours. The textures will vary depending on your baby's development and preferences, but they should be of a thicker and lumpier consistency, and include minced meats or coarsely puréed meat, and minced or soft vegetables.

The transition from one stage to another is gradual and may be slower in premature babies. It is important that babies move beyond puréed and smooth food, to help them develop a feel for different textures, in preparation for family food. Delaying the introduction of new textures for too long may lead to fussiness and the rejection of food without a smooth consistency.

As we introduce new textures to baby's food, encourage baby to develop new motor skills. How do we do this? By offering soft, manageable finger foods! As your baby begins to put more and more things in his mouth, like toys and almost anything within reach, this is the perfect time to allow him to take some control over his eating adventure. Ideal finger foods can include soft, buttered pieces of toast cut into strips; steamed carrot pieces; thin, ripe, peeled pear wedges; and teething biscuits.

A confident baby will feed himself and enjoy it. He will spill and create a mess but this is all part of the learning experience. If you always take control of feeding time, you deprive your child of learning a basic survival skill — self-feeding. Allow your baby to drink fluids from a sippy cup or a baby-safe cup with a straw. Your smart little one will soon learn to eat, and eat enough.

Real Mum Tip: *Do not stress over the mess your baby creates while self-feeding! Give him a chance to learn by touching and feeling all these new foods. If you cannot stand the spills and mess, invest in a splatter mat or put down some old newspaper under your baby's highchair. Being relaxed about the mess results in a happier mum and baby!*

Fluids

At nine to 12 months of age, your baby can be introduced to fluids in a cup. In addition to breast milk or formula milk, water is ideal as it quenches baby's thirst effectively.

The introduction of fruit juice is an issue that remains controversial among nutrition experts. Do babies really need fruit juice if they are getting regular servings of fruit? The general rule that is laced with common sense, is that diluted, 100% fruit juice, can be added to your baby's diet once he can drink from a cup. However, fruit juice should not replace more important fluids such as milk feeds. Another concern regarding juice is the sucking of it from bottles for long periods of time. Dentists, paediatricians and GPs refer to this as "nursing bottle caries" or "nursing bottle syndrome", which means that if your child falls asleep sucking on a bottle of juice (or even milk!), it can cause tooth decay or caries. An excessive amount of juice — more than 250 ml (8 fl oz / 1 cup) — in a baby's diet can also lead to diarrhoea or loose stools.

Limit Salt, Sugar and Spices

For a healthy, growing baby, foods are naturally flavourful, and there is no need for added sodium or sugar in the first year of life.

We all need some sodium in our diet, but we can usually get enough from what is naturally present in the food we eat. Added salt or seasoning is not necessary, as the body has no need for added sodium. In fact, even commercially made baby foods are tightly regulated to restrict sodium levels today.

The use of canned food and other processed foods, which contain high amounts of sodium, is thus not appropriate in the preparation of baby's first foods. Very salty foods like preserved or pickled vegetables and salted meat or fish are also not recommended. Too much sodium can be difficult for a baby's immature kidneys to handle.

Similarly, refrain from sweetening baby's foods with added sugar. Although babies need many nutrients for their rapid rate of growth, and sugar provides calories, it contains no other vitamins or minerals. High sugar foods, such as candies or cookies, are usually low in nutrient density and high in calories, so we should offer them to older babies or toddlers only as occasional treats, and focus on more nutrient dense foods, such as bananas, instead. Realistically, it is virtually impossible to avoid high sugar foods forever, but by monitoring what your child is eating and moderating the amount and frequency of high sugar foods, you can instil good eating habits.

Research has shown that humans exhibit an innate preference to sweet tastes, but interestingly, taste preferences in children are learned and largely influenced by their experiences. Adding sugar masks the natural flavour of food and causes babies to become accustomed to sweeter tastes. This may lead to cultivating a preference for intensely sweetened foods, and excessive intake of sweetened foods, like all other foods, may contribute to obesity. There is also evidence to show that consuming sweet, sticky foods increase the risk of dental caries, so wipe your child's mouth gently with a moistened, soft cloth, if sweet foods are consumed. It is also untrue that natural sweeteners are better for babies. Sugar is still sugar regardless if it is called cane sugar, table sugar, white sugar, brown sugar, jaggery, honey, fructose, sucrose, glucose or corn syrup.

finger foods and one-dish meals

You will either love our next set of recipes or find them challenging. Whichever it is, you must:

- Make eating an adventure. Expand baby's food experiences. Serve up new foods and cook them foods differently. Your naturally curious child will look forward to each new meal that you prepare with love and creativity.

- Remember that your baby can now chew and swallow. Providing a range of textures will give him a chance to use those skills.

- Encourage your baby to start self-feeding. Children can now hold food with fingers or palms. They have also mastered the skill of putting food into the mouth. So, prepare foods that your little one can use to hone these abilities.

Children are smart. They are born with natural skills for survival and one such skill is eating. So, do not take over your child's meal times. Give your child space to learn and develop. For this purpose, we have included recipes for foods that your child can eat with fingers and with a baby spoon.

We are also introducing the concept of one-dish meals. These are more elaborate recipes that resemble family meals. They are convenient to prepare even when you are rushed for time. These recipes include familiar ingredients that you can use when preparing meals for the rest of the family.

Once you have tested these recipes, apply the techniques to modify your favourite recipes to suit your child's abilities. Just be mindful to introduce ingredients that are suited to your child at this stage.

Finger Foods

Whole Wheat Pancake Rolls *Makes 4*

Nutrient Analysis Per roll

Energy 48 kcals
Protein 1 g
Carbohydrates 9 g
Total fat 1 g
Saturated fat 0.7 g
Cholesterol 3 mg
Dietary fibre 1.6 g
Sodium 8 mg
Calcium 5 mg
Iron 0.3 mg

Whole wheat flour *30 g (1 oz / ¼ cup)*
Water *125 ml (4 fl oz / ½ cup)*
Butter or soy oil *1 tsp*
Fruit purée *4 Tbsp*

1   Mix whole wheat flour and water together in a mixing bowl to get a thin batter of pouring consistency.

2   Heat an iron griddle or non-stick frying pan and grease lightly with butter or oil.

3   Pour a ladle of batter (about 3 Tbsp) on the griddle or pan. With the back of the ladle, spread the batter gently to make a small pancake.

4   Cook until you see small bubbles appearing at the edges, then flip the pancake to cook the other side until it is golden brown in colour.

5   Remove the pancake from the pan and leave to cool slightly. Repeat to make 4 pancakes.

6   Spread each pancake with 1 Tbsp fruit purée. Roll up, then slice thinly to serve.

TIPS ❋ Your toddler can be involved in making these pancakes. Let him help mix the batter, spread the purée or simply watch you prepare and cook. Make sure that the hot frying pan is well out of reach of your toddler.

Variation

For extra taste and nutrients, add different ingredients into the plain pancake batter. The rule of thumb is to use about 2 tablespoons of each ingredient per half cup batter. Try these:

- Chopped, cooked pumpkin
- Chopped or mashed ripe avocado
- Chopped or shredded chicken
- Grated mild cheddar cheese
- Apple purée (or any fruit purée)
- Chopped raisins

Baked Beetroot *Makes ¹/₂ cup*

Beetroot may not come immediately to mind when you are selecting fresh vegetables for your little one, but these unheralded gems pack a nutrient punch! Beetroot is high in vitamin C, folate and dietary fibre. With its beautiful, deep red colour, beetroot is also an excellent source of antioxidants. Baking the beetroot slowly will lightly caramelise the vegetable, bringing out its natural sweetness.

Nutrient Analysis
Per ¹/₄ cup serving

Energy 60 kcals
Protein 1 g
Carbohydrates 9 g
Total fat 2 g
Saturated fat 1.2 g
Cholesterol 5 mg
Dietary fibre 0.3 g
Sodium 40 mg
Calcium 70 mg
Iron 1.4 mg

Beetroot *1, small, about 200 g (7 oz)*
Melted butter *1 tsp*

1 Wash the beetroot thoroughly but gently, taking care not to break the skin. Remove the green tops/leaves.

2 Wrap the beetroot with aluminium foil and bake in a preheated oven at 200°C (400°F) for 2 hours. Unwrap the beetroot and immediately place it in a bowl of cold water. Peel off the skin and dice.

3 Toss the diced beetroot in the melted butter and serve warm.

* Choose small or medium-size beetroot, as they tend to be more tender.

* Fresh beetroot should be firm with smooth skin and still have their leaves.

* Cut off the leaves after bringing the beetroot home, as the leaves absorb moisture from the roots. However, leave a small section of the stem intact to prevent nutrient and colour loss.

* Always leave the skin on when cooking beetroot to prevent loss of nutrients and leaching of colour.

* It can be a tricky task to peel cooked beetroot as the colour runs. However, the beetroot stains can be easily washed off fingers.

* Beetroot can also be boiled or steamed.

Variation

Use this recipe to bake other vegetables such sweet potatoes, potatoes, yams, carrots or pumpkins.

One-dish Meals

Sweet Potato, Pork and Liver Porridge

Makes 2 cups

In Asia, liver, is valued as a highly nutritious food. Indeed, animal liver (pig, chicken or calf) is an excellent source of B vitamins, vitamin A, copper, folate and selenium. It is also a good source of protein, zinc and iron. Excessive intake of vitamin A from animal foods, however, can be toxic, and it is best to include liver in your baby's diet only occasionally and in small portions (about two times a week and 2 tablespoonfuls at each occasion).

**Nutrient Analysis
Per $^1/_2$ cup serving**

Energy 201 kcals
Protein 13 g
Carbohydrates 22 g
Total fat 7 g
Saturated fat 2.5 g
Cholesterol 41 mg
Dietary fibre 2.3 g
Sodium 56 mg
Calcium 26 mg
Iron 2.5 mg

Brown rice *50 g ($1^3/_4$ oz / $^1/_4$ cup)*
Sweet potato *250 g (9 oz)*
Homemade stock (pork, chicken or vegetable) *1.25 litres (40 fl oz / 5 cups)*
Minced pork *100 g ($3^1/_2$ oz)*
Pig's liver *30 g (1 oz)*

1 Wash the brown rice and drain, then grind it using a hand-held blender or food processor to a fine consistency.

2 Wash and peel the sweet potato, then cut into small pieces or cubes.

3 Bring the homemade stock to the boil in a pot. Add the ground brown rice and sweet potato. When the stock returns to the boil, reduce heat to allow the porridge to gently simmer for 20 minutes. Stir frequently to prevent the porridge from sticking to the bottom of the pot and burning.

4 Place the minced pork in a small bowl. Add 2 Tbsp warm water and stir to prevent the meat from clumping. Add the meat to the porridge and cook for another 10–15 minutes or until the meat is cooked through. Remove from heat and set the porridge aside to cool a little.

5 Meanwhile, bring 250 ml (8 fl oz / 1 cup) water to the boil in a small pot. Add the liver and cook for 5 minutes. Pierce the liver with a fork to check that it is cooked through before removing from heat. The juices should run clear.

6 Drain and dice the liver finely. Add to the porridge and mix well. Serve warm.

TIPS

✳ Fresh liver is best purchased from the market or a reliable butcher. Use the liver as soon as possible after buying.

✳ For food safety reasons, always cook liver thoroughly.

Chicken and Avocado Delight *Makes 1¼ cups*

Roasted chicken meat *75 g (2½ oz)*
Ripe avocado flesh *65 g (2⅓ oz)*
Apple *40 g (1½ oz / ¼ cup), peeled and cored*
Grated mild cheddar cheese *2 Tbsp*
Plain, full-fat yoghurt *1 Tbsp*

1 Remove the skin of the roasted chicken. Chop the chicken into small cubes.

2 Chop the avocado and apple into small pieces.

3 Place all ingredients, except the yoghurt, in a medium bowl and mix well.

4 Add the yoghurt and gently fold all the ingredients together.

5 Serve as a main dish with rice, potato or bread.

TIPS

∗ If your baby is not ready to handle cubed pieces of chicken, mince it and grate the avocado and apple.

∗ Use homemade yoghurt or select a mild yoghurt suitable for your baby's sensitive palate.

Couscous with Chicken and Vegetables

Makes 1 cup

**Nutrient Analysis
Per ¹/₂ cup serving**

Energy 267 kcals

Protein 13 g

Carbohydrates 29 g

Total fat 11 g

Saturated fat 4.7 g

Cholesterol 21 mg

Dietary fibre 3.7 g

Sodium 122 mg

Calcium 103 mg

Iron 0.9 mg

Butter *2 tsp*

Minced chicken *3 Tbsp, about 45 g (1¹/₂ oz)*

Finely grated carrot *1 Tbsp, about 30 g (1 oz)*

Finely diced cauliflower *1 Tbsp, about 30 g (1 oz)*

Finely diced French beans *1 Tbsp, about 30 g (1 oz)*

Couscous *6 Tbsp, about 60 g (2 oz)*

Homemade stock (see pages 82–84) *150 ml (5 fl oz)*

Grated cheese *2 Tbsp, about 20 g (²/₃ oz)*

1   Melt butter in a small pan over low heat.

2   Add minced chicken, carrot, cauliflower and French beans. Cook for
10 minutes or until chicken is cooked through and vegetables are tender.

3   Add couscous, stir and cook for another 1 minute.

4   Add stock and stir well so that the couscous absorbs the water and
achieves a smooth consistency.

5   Garnish with cheese and serve warm.

Variation

Use flaked fish instead of minced chicken for this recipe. The couscous can
also be substituted with semolina, which is available from some supermarkets and
Indian grocery stores.

Mee Sua with Egg Yolk and Spinach *Makes 1 cup*

Babies nine months or older can be introduced to egg yolks. Eggs are truly one of nature's super foods, and most of the nutrients are found in the yolk. Egg yolk contains carotenes, essential fatty acids, choline, vitamins A, E, D and K. It is also a source of B vitamins, calcium, iron, phosphorus, zinc and folate. Chickens fed special diets can produce eggs that are rich in omega-3 essential fatty acid, and such eggs can be found in most supermarkets.

While dietary guidelines for adults recommend the consumption of no more than three to four egg yolks per week, there are no specific guidelines for children. Babies can handle cholesterol as it is found in breast milk as well. In fact, babies need cholesterol for optimal growth because it is an integral part of cell structure, especially nerve cells. Egg whites should only be given to babies 12 months or older, as they are known to be more allergenic than egg yolks.

Nutrient Analysis
Per ½ cup serving

Energy 131 kcals
Protein 7 g
Carbohydrates 17 g
Total fat 4 g
Saturated fat 1 g
Cholesterol 103 mg
Dietary fibre 1 g
Sodium 122 mg
Calcium 56 mg
Iron 2 mg

Water *500 ml (16 fl oz / 2 cups)*
Mee sua (fine wheat noodles) *45 g (1½ oz)*
Soy bean oil *½ tsp*
Egg yolk *1, lightly beaten until smooth*
Chye sim or spinach *50 g (1¾ oz)*
Homemade stock (see pages 82–84) *375 ml (12 fl oz / 1½ cups)*

1 Bring the water to the boil in a small pot. Blanch the *mee sua* for 2 minutes, then drain and rinse with cold water. Cut the *mee sua* into small pieces and set aside.

2 Heat the oil in a small frying pan. Add the beaten egg yolk and scramble it using a wooden spatula. Set the scrambled egg yolk aside.

3 Wash and drain the vegetables. Pluck the leaves and discard the stems. Chop the leaves up finely.

4 Bring the homemade stock to the boil in a pot. Add the vegetables and *mee sua* and cook for 5 minutes or until the vegetables are soft and cooked.

5 Transfer the *mee sua* soup to a small bowl and top with the scrambled egg yolk. Allow it to cool a little before serving.

Alphabet Pasta *Makes 1 cup cooked pasta and 1½ cups sauce*

Gradually introduce red meat, such as lean cuts of beef and lamb that have been minced or puréed, to baby after nine months of age. Your first few attempts may be rejected due to the stronger flavour and coarser texture of red meat, but do not give up. Red meat is a good source of protein, minerals such as zinc and phosphorous, as well as many of the B vitamins. Importantly, red meat is rich in iron, which baby needs to produce red blood cells and to boost cognitive development.

With natural sweetness from the vegetables, a slight tang from the tomatoes and meaty flavours from the beef, this delicious dish will satisfy baby's growing appetite.

**Nutrient Analysis
Per ½ cup serving**

Energy 94 kcals
Protein 3 g
Carbohydrates 7 g
Total fat 6 g
Saturated fat 1.7 g
Cholesterol 10 mg
Dietary fibre 0.9 g
Sodium 15 mg
Calcium 11 mg
Iron 0.6 mg

Alphabet pasta *50 g (1¾ oz / 1½ cup)*
Carrot *30 g (1 oz)*
White onion *30 g (1 oz)*
Yellow capsicum (bell pepper) *30 g (1 oz)*
Fresh ripe tomatoes or canned tomatoes *150 g (5⅓ oz)*
Olive or soy bean oil *1 Tbsp*
Puréed or finely minced beef *60 g (2 oz)*
Courgette (zucchini) *30 g (1 oz)*
Homemade vegetable stock (see pages 82–84) or water *250 ml (8 fl oz / 1 cup)*

1 Cook pasta according to package directions. When pasta is cooked and soft, drain and set aside.

2 Wash, peel and finely dice the carrot, onion and courgette. Wash, seed and finely dice the capsicum and tomatoes. If using canned tomatoes, dice finely.

3 Heat the oil in a pan and add the carrot, onion, capsicum and tomatoes. Cook for 10 minutes or until tender.

4 Add the puréed or minced beef and courgette and cook for another 10 minutes, stirring to mix well.

5 Add the homemade vegetable stock or water, and simmer for a further 10 minutes. Remove from heat and add the cooked pasta. Stir to mix well.

6 Allow the pasta and the sauce to cool a little before serving.

 TIPS ✳ Use other fine pasta, such as angel hair pasta, cut into small pieces.

Steamed Tofu Cubes with Mango Sauce

Makes 1 cup

Tofu is made by coagulating hot soy milk with calcium salts. It is a rich source of protein. In fact, soy is the one plant protein that, like animal protein foods, has all the essential amino acids needed to support growth. It is also a good source of calcium and a fair source of iron.

Tofu is such a baby-friendly food. You can cube it, dice it or mash it, and serve with a tasty sauce or soup to make a main dish. Choose from the range of different tofu textures available and find one that suits your recipe. This versatile ingredient also makes a delicious dessert when served with a fruit sauce, or a wonderful baby beverage when blended with fruit.

Nutrient Analysis
Per ¼ cup serving

Energy 82 kcals

Protein 3 g

Carbohydrates 13 g

Total fat 2 g

Saturated fat 0.3 g

Cholesterol 0 mg

Dietary fibre 1.4 g

Sodium 5 mg

Calcium 49 mg

Iron 0.5 mg

Silken tofu *150 g (5⅓ oz)*
Ripe mango *1 small, about 300 g (11 oz)*

1 Cut the tofu into little cubes, then steam and set aside.

2 Remove the skin and stone of mango, then cut the flesh into small cubes. Place half the mango cubes in a blender or food processor and purée. Set aside.

3 Arrange the tofu and mango cubes in a large bowl. Drizzle with mango purée and serve.

✳ Choose a sweet, ripe mango for this recipe.

✳ Cooked apple and pear purées or fresh papaya purée also make delicious sweet sauces to serve with tofu.

Baked Fish with Citrus Sauce *Makes ³/₄ cup*

White fish fillet (eg. red snapper or cod fish) *1, about 150 g (5¹/₃ oz)*

Butter *1 Tbsp*

Freshly-squeezed orange juice or store-bought orange juice
  with no added sugar *60 ml (2 fl oz / ¹/₄ cup)*

1 Preheat the oven to 180°C (350°F).

2 Remove all bones from the fish fillet, then place the fillet in a shallow baking dish or roasting pan.

3 Cut the butter into small pieces.

4 Pour the orange juice over the fish and sprinkle with pieces of butter. Cover with aluminium foil and bake for about 20 minutes.

5 Allow the fish to cool slightly before flaking the flesh with a fork and serving serving.

* If pressed for time, place the ingredients in a microwave-safe dish and microwave on high for 2 to 3 minutes, or until the fish is cooked through and the flesh flakes easily when pricked with a fork.

... is my favorite food.

beyond purées and porridges

1 through 2 years of age

Happy 1st Birthday! After the great milestone of your baby's first birthday, life opens up for your baby-turned-toddler! Your toddler is now able to handle more variety, texture, finger foods and even, family food. Even though it is a busy time in your household, it is important to create family time together around a meal. This will show your child that eating is an enjoyable and social part of life and family.

Cultivating Healthy Eating Behaviours

Health experts recommend that food should not be used as a reward or bribe for good behaviour or for preventing bad ones. We may recall hearing the familiar words, "If you finish your dinner, you can have dessert", during our childhood, or seen some exasperated parent in the grocery store giving in to their child saying, "I will buy you that candy if you just stop screaming." When faced with such behaviours, it is easy to find a quick way out that will appease both parent and child, but this often leads to worsening behaviour further encouraged by food bribes or food rewards. It also teaches the child that there are 'good' and 'bad' foods, which is not true. All foods, even treats, can fit into a healthy diet. We just want to choose the healthier ones more often and the not-so-healthy ones less often!

Desserts and candy can be built into a healthy meal pattern, when offered in small portions and on special occasions only. So, the next time you want to reward your child for good behaviour, offer sincere praise, a hug or spend quality time together doing fun things like singing, reading a book or just playing. If your child throws a tantrum, be firm. Give clear and simple directions to calm your child. Repeat yourself if necessary, but do not give in. If you do, your child will not respect your instructions the next time around. If necessary, send your child to bed or to his room to spend a little time to calm down.

Children do not have the knowledge to make healthy food choices, so they depend on you, the parent, to offer healthy and varied food choices. This provides them with a foundation of good eating habits, even in the fussiest eater. While we know that picky eaters can be frustrating and difficult to please, being relaxed about meal times and consistently offering healthy food options provides the best long-term solution.

Eat at least one meal with your toddler every day. Allow your child to sit at the family table. Children model behaviours by watching adults. Be a role model, eat a well-balanced diet made of healthier food choices and demonstrate good table manners. Soon, your child will have a healthy attitude towards food and eating.

Encourage Self-feeding Skills

Your little one should have now moved on from purées through porridges and made the transition to finger foods and bite-size portions. His food should include a wide variety of textures — some soft, and others that encourage biting and chewing. While your toddler still has some way to go to handle family foods, the confidence he has with basic skills, will facilitate quick learning. Good chewing skills encourage proper jaw formation, good development of teeth and can even impact speech as well.

Your child should now be able to drink from a cup and eat with fingers and even, a spoon. He should be allowed to eat by himself, with some supervision from an adult, at meal times. By allowing your child the opportunity to develop and fine-tune these skills, he will soon be able to handle a fork and even a pair of chopsticks!

Continue to supervise and guide your child's eating, but do not feed him. Remember to seat your toddler down at each meal, and help him to focus on eating. In this way, your toddler will develop responsible eating habits. Avoid running after him with a bowl of food or feeding him in front of the television or while reading a book.

Food Variety

Your toddler should now be eating foods from all the foods groups — grains, fruit, vegetables, meat and dairy. Continue to provide a variety each day to start building up a balanced diet. Continue to breast feed, if you can, or offer at least three milk feeds a day. As your child's appetite improves, build toward regular meal times of breakfast, lunch and dinner, with snacks in between.

Your child should now be able to eat family foods from the table as long as they are not too spicy or strongly flavoured. If you have no history of allergy in the family, you can begin to introduce egg whites, whole eggs, seafood, soy and nuts that you have been holding back on. However, continue using the same rule of one new food for three days to identify adverse reactions, if any.

Cow's Milk

While you are encouraged to continue breastfeeding your toddler, after 12 months, pasteurised cow's milk can now be introduced into his diet. Cow's milk is a good source of bone-building calcium and provides other important nutrients like vitamin D, protein and phosphorus.

food glorious food!

After a very interesting first year, your toddler is now equipped with tremendous skills. Chewing and swallowing foods; picking up foods with fingers; and even managing a spoon, expertly directing delectable portions from the bowl to the mouth.

Enjoy the next leg of the journey. You are in charge. Expand your child's food horizons and continue to introduce new food and dishes. Use this opportunity to introduce foods from different cultures, so that your little one will fearlessly eat from a variety of foods.

Talk to your child about the goodness of food. Use stories, cartoons and even songs to educate him about the nourishing benefits of different foods.

Involve your child in the preparation of family food. Take a walk in your home garden, or make a visit to a local farm and show your child how plants grow, and even let him water them. Take your child to the market and help him learn the names of vegetables and fruit. Let your little one watch you prepare foods as well. This approach will make food and eating a family activity and solidify the foundation of healthy eating in the future.

Be a role model when it comes to eating by selecting healthier foods, practising healthy eating behaviours and demonstrating eating etiquette. Your child learns best by imitating you.

This set of recipes involves family foods seasoned to taste with herbs, some spices and a little soy sauce, salt and sugar. We focus on making foods flavourful so that eating is fun for your child. Many of our recipes are adult-friendly as well and can be scaled up to make family meals.

Here we introduce cow's milk and whole eggs to your toddler's diet. Until your child turns two, use whole, full-fat milk. If your baby is allergic to or intolerant to cow's milk, use calcium-fortified soy milk or rice milk as substitutes in these recipes.

Breakfast to Start the day

French Toast *Makes 4 slices*

Eggs are a great source of protein. The quality of protein in egg is considered to be of high biological value — it is absorbed and utilised effectively. Whole eggs are also a good source of several B vitamins, a fair amount of vitamin A and some iron. Unlike egg yolks, egg whites are low in calories and free of cholesterol. If your child is allergic to eggs, however, avoid them.

Nutrient Analysis Per ½ slice each of wholemeal and raisin French toast

Energy 128 kcals
Protein 6 g
Carbohydrates 16 g
Total fat 5 g
Saturated fat 2.6 g
Cholesterol 62 mg
Dietary fibre 1.5 g
Sodium 147 mg
Calcium 78 mg
Iron 1.2 mg

Butter *2 tsp*
Egg *1, about 50 g (1³/₄ oz)*
Whole milk *125 ml (4 fl oz / 1 ½ cup)*
Soft wholemeal bread *2 slices, about 50 g (1³/₄ oz)*
Raisin bread *2 slices, about 60 g (2 oz)*

1 Melt the butter in a small pan over low heat. Do not allow the butter to burn. Pour the melted butter into a large bowl and allow it to cool slightly.

2 Crack the egg into another bowl and beat lightly.

3 Add the milk and beaten egg to the melted butter.

4 Remove the crusts from the slices of bread and cut the bread into small pieces. Alternatively, cut the bread into fun shapes using cookie cutters.

5 Dip the bread pieces, one at a time, into the egg and milk mixture until well coated.

6 Heat a non-stick pan over medium-high heat. Add the bread pieces and cook until both sides are golden brown.

7 Allow the bread to cool before serving.

TIPS

* Check that the French toast is cool enough before serving to your toddler as the centre can still be very hot.

* This can be served as is, or with a small amount of fruit purée or maple syrup for added sweetness.

Creamy Carrot Soup *Makes 2 cups*

Soups are a great way to deliver water and a wide range of nutrients to your toddler. If your toddler does not enjoy vegetables, then cook it up and blend it to make a rich and nourishing soup. Many children fuss with vegetable pieces served on their own, but, when cooked in a flavourful broth, they eat it up with ease.

Nutrient Analysis Per ¹/₂ cup

Energy 66 kcals
Protein 2 g
Carbohydrates 7 g
Total fat 4 g
Saturated fat 2.2 g
Cholesterol 9 mg
Dietary fibre 1.6 g
Sodium 62 mg
Calcium 37 mg
Iron 0.2 mg

Carrots *2, medium, about 250 g (9 oz)*
White onion *¹/₂, about 50 g (1³/₄ oz)*
Butter *1 Tbsp*
Whole milk *60 ml (2 fl oz / ¹/₄ cup)*
Homemade chicken stock (see page 82) *250 ml (4 fl oz / 1 cup)*

1 Wash and peel the carrots, then cut them into medium-size pieces.

2 Peel and chop the onion.

3 Melt the butter in a large saucepan over medium heat. Add the onion and cook until soft.

4 Add the carrots and cook for about 10 minutes.

5 Add the homemade chicken stock, then cover the saucepan with a lid and bring to the boil.

6 When the stock comes to the boil, reduce heat and allow the stock to simmer for 15–20 minutes or until the carrots are soft.

7 Remove from heat and allow to cool slightly.

8 Purée the mixture in batches using a hand-held blender or food processor. Place the puréed soup in a bowl.

9 Warm the milk in a small pan over low heat, then add it to the purée and stir to mix well.

10 Serve the soup with small bread sticks for dipping.

* This soup can be made the night before and kept in the refrigerator. Warm it up before serving.

* Vary the vegetables to make other delicious soups. Use broccoli, peas, spinach or pumpkin.

Breakfast Scramble *Makes ¹/₂ cup*

This is one easy recipe that takes less than 10 minutes to whip up. With a little bit of imagination, you can whip up a stronger flavoured version for adults (using additional vegetables or smoked salmon), while preparing a milder and wholesome breakfast suitable for your toddler.

Nutrient Analysis Per ¹/₄ cup

Energy 85 kcals
Protein 4 g
Carbohydrates 2 g
Total fat 7 g
Saturated fat 3.2 g
Cholesterol 117 mg
Dietary fibre 0.2 g
Sodium 69 mg
Calcium 50 mg
Iron 0.6 mg

Button mushroom *1, about 10 g (¹/₃ oz)*
Ripe tomato *1, about 30 g (1 oz)*
Egg *1, about 50 g (1³/₄ oz)*
Whole milk *60 ml (2 fl oz / ¹/₄ cup)*
Butter *¹/₂ Tbsp*

1 Wash and drain the mushroom, then chop into small pieces.

2 Wash and deseed the tomato, then chop into small pieces.

3 Crack the egg into a small bowl and add the milk. Using a fork, beat the egg and milk mixture lightly with a fork until well-combined.

4 Melt the butter in a saucepan over low heat. Add the mushroom and tomato and stir-fry for 2 minutes.

5 Add the egg and milk mixture, and scramble it using a wooden spatula.

6 When the egg has cooked through, remove the pan from heat and place the scrambled egg on a plate.

7 Serve with strips of soft toast or pancake.

 TIPS

※ Serve the scramble on its own with soft bread or in a sandwich for travelling convenience.

※ Vary the vegetables. Add cheese and even a little cooked, shredded meat for interest.

Assorted Bread Roll-Ups *Makes 3 servings*

The ultimate convenience food, the sandwich is a must-have in childhood.
Start with simple, easy-to-use fillings and then, build in a greater variety.
Serve it in the classic closed sandwich style, as a roll, or an open-face toast.

Sandwiches bring together the goodness of a variety of healthy ingredients.
The bread supplies complex carbohydrates and fibre. Fruit spreads add useful
minerals like potassium and are free of sugar. Protein-rich fillings include egg,
cheese, peanut butter, chicken, tuna and beef. Start adding vegetables to the
fillings — sliced or chopped tomato, cucumber and lettuce — so your child
learns to accept and enjoy these healthy foods.

**Nutrient Analysis
Per serving**

Energy 104 kcals
Protein 4 g
Carbohydrates 13 g
Total fat 4 g
Saturated fat 2.5 g
Cholesterol 14 mg
Dietary fibre 0.9 g
Sodium 128 mg
Calcium 42 mg
Iron 0.9 mg

Soft wholemeal bread *1 slice, about 25 g (⁴/₅ oz)*
White bread *1 slice, about 25 g (⁴/₅ oz)*
Plain full-fat yoghurt *2 Tbsp*
Tuna canned in water *30 g (1 oz), drained and flaked*
Cream cheese *2 Tbsp*
Peach half, canned in juice *1, about 70 g (2¹/₂ oz), drained and thinly sliced*
Cucumber *15 g (¹/₂ oz), peeled and thinly sliced*

1 Trim the crusts from the bread slices. Flatten the bread slightly with a rolling pin,
then cut each slice of bread lengthwise into 3 equal pieces.

2 Place the yoghurt in a small bowl and add the flaked tuna, mixing well.

3 Spread the tuna and yoghurt filling on a slice of white bread and top with cucumber
slices. Roll up.

4 Spread the cream cheese on a slice of wholemeal bread and top with some peach
slices. Roll up.

5 Serve 1 peach and cream cheese roll-up and 1 tuna and cucumber roll-up as 1 serving.

＊ Bread, butter and jam is a classic combination. Use unsweetened jams or fruit purées
for healthier spreads.

＊ An egg sandwich or peanut butter sandwich also make healthy breakfast items and
substantial snacks.

Main Meals

Cod with Sweet Corn Sauce on Rice *Makes 2 cups*

Cod has a soft texture that many children enjoy. It is high in protein, rich in vitamin B_{12}, a good source of niacin, vitamin B6 and magnesium. It also has some valuable omega-3 fatty acids. This ultimate comfort food combines the goodness of vegetables and fish in a delicious corn sauce served with warm rice.

Nutrient Analysis Per 1/2 cup

Energy 134 kcals
Protein 7 g
Carbohydrates 13 g
Total fat 6 g
Saturated fat 0.9 g
Cholesterol 11 mg
Dietary fibre 1.9 g
Sodium 83 mg
Calcium 15 mg
Iron 0.4 mg

Cod fish fillet *100 g (3¹/₂ oz)*
Frozen corn kernels *60 g (2 oz / ¹/₄ cup)*
French beans *60 g (2 oz / ¹/₄ cup)*
Soy bean oil *1¹/₂ Tbsp*
Canned cream corn *65 g (2¹/₃ oz / ¹/₄ cup)*
Light soy sauce *¹/₂ tsp*
Water *2 Tbsp*
Cooked brown or white rice *100 g (3¹/₂ oz / ¹/₂ cup)*

1 Remove all bones from the cod fish fillet.

2 Place the frozen corn kernels in a bowl and leave to thaw a little.

3 Wash and dice the French beans.

4 Heat 1 Tbsp oil in a saucepan and add the cod fillet. Pan-fry over low heat for 10 minutes or until just golden brown and cooked through. Place in a bowl and set aside.

5 In the same saucepan, heat the remaining ¹/₂ Tbsp oil. Add the diced French beans and stir-fry for 2 minutes. Add the cream corn, corn kernels, light soy sauce and water. Cook for another 5 minutes or until sauce is of desired consistency. Remove from heat and allow to cool a little.

6 Spoon the rice into the bowl with the cod fish, and top with the corn sauce.

✳ Replace the cod fish with other fatty fish like salmon or mackerel.

✳ A thickened soup stock can also be used instead of cream corn.

Tomato Vermicelli _Makes 2¹/₂ cups_

Vermicelli can be made with rice or wheat. Rice vermicelli cooks quickly but wheat vermicelli, like all other pastas, takes a little longer, about 8–10 minutes. Thin wheat vermicelli can be found in most Indian specialty stores.

Nutrient Analysis Per ¹/₂ cup

Energy 145 kcals
Protein 4 g
Carbohydrates 19 g
Total fat 6 g
Saturated fat 0.9 g
Cholesterol 0 mg
Dietary fibre 1.5 g
Sodium 62 mg
Calcium 17 mg
Iron 1 mg

Soy bean oil _2 Tbsp_
Thin wheat vermicelli _100 g (3¹/₂ oz)_
Finely chopped onion _100 g (3¹/₂ oz)_
Ground cinnamon _a pinch_
Ground cloves _a pinch_
Ground cardamom _a pinch_
Finely chopped ginger _¹/₂ tsp_
Finely chopped garlic _1 tsp_
Ripe tomatoes _2, small, about 200 g (7 oz), washed, deseeded and chopped_
Courgette (zucchini) _60 g (2 oz), washed, peeled and grated_
Homemade chicken or vegetable stock (see pages **82** and **84**) _125 ml (4 fl oz / ¹/₂ cup)_
Salt (optional) _¹/₈ tsp_
Chopped coriander leaves (cilantro) _1 Tbsp_

1   Heat the oil in a frying pan and fry the vermicelli for 5–10 minutes or until golden brown. Remove from the pan and set aside.

2   In the same pan, heat more oil and fry the onion, spices, ginger and garlic for 5–10 minutes or until fragrant.

3   Add the tomatoes and cook well for 10 minutes or until tomatoes are very soft. Add the cooked vermicelli and grated courgette and stir to combine all ingredients.

4   Gradually add the stock a little at a time, and continue to cook for another 10–15 minutes or until vermicelli is well done. Season with salt if needed.

5   Garnish with coriander and allow to cool before serving.

Variation

This is a vegetarian recipe, but feel free to add some protein foods such as shredded chicken or lean meat slices to make it a more complete meal. If you are vegetarian, add tofu cubes or cottage cheese to boost the protein content of this dish.

Rainbow Rice *Makes 2 cups*

This is another delicious one-dish meal that is a hit with young ones. It cleverly combines the flavours of meat with vegetables cooked in stock and is served over warm rice. Even fussy vegetable eaters will appreciate this tasty meal. It is also a nutritional winner as it provides energy, protein and a host of vitamins, minerals and fibre.

Nutrient Analysis Per $^1/_2$ cup

Energy 119 kcals
Protein 5 g
Carbohydrates 9 g
Total fat 7 g
Saturated fat 2 g
Cholesterol 64 mg
Dietary fibre 1.2 g
Sodium 190 mg
Calcium 15 mg
Iron 0.7 mg

Soy bean oil *1 Tbsp*
Frozen mixed vegetables *65 g (2$^1/_3$ oz / $^1/_3$ cup)*
Minced beef or pork *50 g (1$^3/_4$ oz / $^1/_4$ cup)*
Homemade stock (see pages 82–84) or water *65 ml (2 fl oz / $^1/_4$ cup)*
Light soy sauce *$^1/_2$ tsp*
Cornflour (cornstarch) *1 tsp, mixed with 1 Tbsp water*
Egg *1, about 50 g (1$^3/_4$ oz)*
Cooked brown or white rice *100 g (3$^1/_2$ oz / 1 cup)*

1   Heat $^1/_2$ Tbsp oil in a saucepan and stir-fry mixed vegetables for 5 minutes.

2   Add the minced meat, homemade stock or water and light soy sauce. Stir-fry for another 5 minutes or until the meat is cooked through. Add the cornflour mixture to thicken the sauce.

3   Place the meat and vegetable sauce in a bowl and allow to cool a little.

4   Crack the egg into a small bowl and beat lightly using a fork.

5   In the same saucepan, heat the remaining $^1/_2$ Tbsp oil. Add the egg and make a thin omelette. When the egg is cooked, remove from heat and set aside to cool a little. Cut into thin strips.

6   Place the cooked rice in a bowl, spoon the meat sauce over and garnish with the egg strips. Decorate the dish as desired before serving.

Noodles in Seafood Soup *Makes 4 cups*

If there is no history of allergy in the family, you can now introduce seafood, one variety at a time, to increase the range of food your child can eat. Prawns are a great source of protein like other popular seafood. It also provides generous amounts of vitamin B_{12} and quite a lot of iron, niacin and heart healthy omega-3 fats.

Nutrient Analysis Per ¾ cup

Energy 109 kcals
Protein 10 g
Carbohydrates 15 g
Total fat 1 g
Saturated fat 0.2 g
Cholesterol 36 mg
Dietary fibre 1.5 g
Sodium 187 mg
Calcium 24 mg
Iron 1 mg

Thin noodles *100 g (3½ oz / 1½ cup)*
Water *1 litre (32 fl oz / 4 cups)*
Fresh grey prawns *8 medium, about 100 g (3½ oz)*
Dried Chinese mushrooms *4, about 20 g (⅔ oz)*
Long Chinese cabbage leaves *30 g (1 oz)*
Homemade stock (see pages 82–84) *1 litre (32 fl oz / 4 cups)*
Grated carrot *30 g (1 oz)*

1   Cut the noodles into short lengths, about 2.5–5 cm (1–2-in).

2   Bring the water to the boil in a pot. When the water is boiling well, add the noodles and cook according to the package directions. When the noodles are ready, drain and set aside.

3   Wash and peel the prawns. Discard the heads. Chop the prawns into small pieces.

4   Wash the dried mushrooms and soak them in a bowl of warm water for 10 minutes. Drain and cut into thin strips.

5   Wash the cabbage leaves and chop into thin strips. Set aside.

6   Bring the homemade stock to the boil. Add the vegetables and cook for 5 minutes or until the vegetables are soft.

7   Add the noodles, mushrooms and prawns, and cook for 5 minutes or until the prawns are cooked through. Remove from heat, and cool a little before serving.

*   You can further boost the protein content of this dish by adding a beaten egg at Step 7, just before the dish is ready. Slowly pour in one beaten egg while stirring continuously.

*   Create variety by using the different types of thin noodles available, such fine Shanghai noodles, thin *kway teow* (flat rice noodles) or thin Japanese soba.

Pan-fried Fish *Makes 2 servings (1 serving = 30 g (1 oz) fish)*

This recipe is a favourite in many Asian homes. The use of mild herbs and spices introduces your little one to the more complex flavours of traditional Asian cuisine. Easy to prepare and cook, it can also be a main entrée in a meal. Marinate extra fish slices and freeze in small portions, so that it can be defrosted for quick meals.

Nutrient Analysis Per serving

Energy 69 kcals
Protein 6 g
Carbohydrates 0 g
Total fat 5 g
Saturated fat 0.7 g
Cholesterol 0 mg
Dietary fibre 0.1 g
Sodium 161 mg
Calcium 5 mg
Iron 0.4 mg

Fish fillet (Spanish makerel (*ikan tenggiri*) or
  threadfin (*ikan kurau*)) *2 pieces, about 60 g (2 oz)*
Salt (optional) *$^1/_8$ tsp*
Ground turmeric *$^1/_{10}$ tsp*
Ground white pepper *$^1/_{10}$ tsp*
Finely minced ginger *$^1/_{10}$ tsp*
Finely minced garlic *$^1/_{10}$ tsp*
Soy bean oil *2 tsp*

1   Remove all bones from the fish fillets.

2   Combine the salt, turmeric, pepper, ginger and garlic in a small bowl and stir well.

3   Rub the spices onto the fish fillets, then cover with plastic wrap (cling film) and set aside to marinate for 30 minutes in the refrigerator.

4   Heat the oil in a non-stick pan. Add the fish and pan-fry for 5–10 minutes or until the fish is cooked on the inside and crispy on the outside.

5   Serve with vegetables and rice, or with bread.

Baked Macaroni with Cheese and Vegetables

Makes 3 servings (1 serving = ¹/₂ cup)

Made with milk, cheese and broccoli, this recipe is a calcium whopper. Calcium is essential for strong bones and teeth. This dish will encourage your baby to chew and develop those jaw muscles!

**Nutrient Analysis
Per serving**

Energy 212 kcals

Protein 11 g

Carbohydrates 22 g

Total fat 9 g

Saturated fat 5.6 g

Cholesterol 28 mg

Dietary fibre 1.6 g

Sodium 158 mg

Calcium 240 mg

Iron 1.1 mg

Frozen mixed vegetables *40 g (1¹/₂ oz / ¹/₄ cup)*

Broccoli florets *25 g (1 oz / ¹/₄ cup)*

Alphabet pasta or small elbow macaroni *60 g (2 oz / ¹/₂ cup)*

Finely grated mild cheese (Cheddar or mozzarella) *60 g (2 oz)*

Fresh whole milk *250 ml (8 fl oz / 1 cup)*

Ground black pepper *¹/₈ tsp*

1 Preheat the oven to 175°C (350°F).

2 Place the frozen mixed vegetables in a bowl and set aside to thaw a little.

3 Using a small saucepan, add enough water to cover the bottom of the pan. Place the broccoli florets in the saucepan and steam for 10 minutes or until tender. Remove from heat and set aside.

4 Cook the pasta according to the package directions. When the pasta is ready, drain and place in a large bowl.

5 Add two-thirds of the grated cheese to the pasta and stir to mix well.

6 In a small saucepan, heat the milk over medium heat until hot. Takes 1–2 minutes. Add the milk to the pasta and cheese mixture, and season with a pinch of pepper. Simmer over low heat, stirring constantly until the sauce thickens.

7 Add the steamed broccoli florets and mixed vegetables to the pasta and cheese. Stir to mix well.

8 Pour the mixture into a small glass or ceramic baking dish. Sprinkle the remaining grated cheese over the top and bake for 15 minutes or until top is lightly browned.

9 Allow to cool for 5–10 minutes. Decorate the dish as desired before serving.

 TIPS

＊ Pasta absorbs moisture rapidly. If the dish seems dry, add a little extra milk, stir well, heat and serve.

144

Sweet and Sour Meatballs *Makes 24 meatballs and $^1/_2$ cup sauce*

These meatballs are rich in protein to support baby's growing muscles, and also a great source of iron, zinc and many B vitamins.

Nutrient Analysis Per serving of 3 meatballs

Energy 79 kcals
Protein 6 g
Carbohydrates 6 g
Total fat 3 g
Saturated fat 0.5 g
Cholesterol 18 mg
Dietary fibre 0.6 g
Sodium 232 mg
Calcium 9 mg
Iron 0.5 mg

Meatballs

Minced meat (beef, pork or chicken) *200 g (7 oz / 1 cup)*
White onion *20 g ($^2/_3$ oz), peeled and finely chopped*
Red apple *30 g (1 oz), washed, peeled, cored and finely chopped*
French beans *15 g ($^1/_2$ oz), washed and finely chopped*
Carrot *15 g ($^1/_2$ oz), washed and finely chopped*
Light soy sauce *1 Tbsp*
Ground white pepper *$^1/_4$ tsp*
Plain (all-purpose) flour *2 Tbsp*
Olive or soy bean oil *2 Tbsp*

Sweet and Sour Sauce

Cooking oil *1 tsp*
Large onion *20 g ($^2/_3$ oz)*
Tomato *60 g (2 oz), washed and finely chopped*
Low sodium tomato sauce *45 g (1$^1/_2$ oz)*
Plum sauce *15 g ($^1/_2$ oz)*
Sugar *7.5 g ($^1/_2$ Tbsp)*
Salt *$^1/_2$ tsp*
Water *60 ml (2 fl oz / $^1/_4$ cup)*
Cornflour (cornstarch) *1 tsp, mixed with 1 tsp water*

1. Mix the meat, onion, apple, French beans, carrot, soy sauce, pepper and plain flour in a mixing bowl until well-combined. Form the mixture into 24 small balls.

2. Heat olive or soy bean oil in a pan and pan-fry meatballs in batches. Fry each batch for about 10 minutes, turning them occasionally, until browned and cooked through.

3. Using a clean pan, prepare sauce. Heat the oil and fry onion lightly until translucent and soft. Add tomato, tomato sauce, plum sauce, sugar, salt and water. Stir to combine.

4. Thicken sauce with corn flour mixture and bring to the boil. Remove from heat and pour sauce into a bowl.

5. Serve meatballs with rice or small pasta shells, and sauce on the side. Cut meatballs into smaller pieces for younger toddlers.

 TIPS

* To store, refrigerate meatballs and sauce separately.

Treats

Food nourishes and eating is a pleasure. We socialise around food. Most traditions call for special foods to be prepared and eaten on feast days and celebrations. What about cakes, cookies, candies, pastries, fries and crisps? Soon, your inquisitive toddler will discover their existence. Banning treats is not the way to go. Prepare your child for the real world by setting family boundaries on treats. Teach your child that treats are to be eaten on special occasions and in small portions, and be a role model! Make sure you offer your child healthy food most of the time, and build in treats sparingly. This way, your child will learn healthy eating habits.

Here are some treats you can build into a healthy diet for your toddler. Enjoy!

First Birthday Cake *Makes one 8-inch round cake, or 12 small cupcakes*

This recipe makes a light and soft fairy cake that is a fantastic base for more elaborate toppings.

Nutrient Analysis Per cupcake

Energy 148 kcals
Protein 2 g
Carbohydrates 16 g
Total fat 9 g
Saturated fat 5.2 g
Cholesterol 56 mg
Dietary fibre 0.1 g
Sodium 133 mg
Calcium 27 mg
Iron 0.4 mg

Butter *125 g (4^1/$_2$ oz / ^{1}/$_2$ cup), softened at room temperature*
Castor (superfine) sugar *165 g (5^2/$_3$ oz / 1 cup)*
Eggs *2, about 100 g (3^1/$_2$ oz), lightly beaten*
Vanilla essence *1 tsp*
Self-raising flour *190 g (6^2/$_3$ oz / 1^1/$_2$ cup)*
Milk *125 ml (4 fl oz / ^{1}/$_2$ cup)*

1. Preheat the oven to 190°C (370°F). Line a 20-cm (8-in) round cake tin with greaseproof paper, or a 12-hole cupcake tin with paper cases.

2. Beat the softened butter and sugar in a medium mixing bowl until pale and fluffy. (Use an electric cake mixer or a wooden spoon).

3. Gradually add the eggs, whisking at the same time to combine well. Add the vanilla essence and stir.

4. Sift the flour into the batter and fold in carefully. Gradually add the milk until the mixture is well combined.

5. Spoon the batter into the prepared cake tin or cupcake tin. Bake the large cake for about 30 minutes and the cupcakes for 20 minutes or until golden brown on top. A bamboo skewer inserted into the centre of the cake(s) should come out clean.

6. Remove from the oven and allow to cool before lifting out from the baking tin.

Basic Butter Icing *Makes about 1 cup*

This basic butter icing is a simple and delicious topping for the birthday cake.

**Nutrient Analysis
Per 1 Tbsp**

Energy 79 *kcals*
Protein 0 *g*
Carbohydrates 13 *g*
Total fat 3 *g*
Saturated fat 2 *g*
Cholesterol 8 *mg*
Dietary fibre 0 *g*
Sodium 2 *mg*
Calcium 4 *mg*
Iron 0 *mg*

Unsalted butter *60 g (2 oz / $1/4$ cup)*
Icing (confectioner's) sugar *250 g (9 oz / 2 cups)*
Milk *3 Tbsp*
Vanilla essence *1 tsp*

1   Cream the butter, then gradually add the icing sugar, alternating with the milk. Beat well after each addition.

2   Stir in the vanilla essence. The icing is ready to be spread on cakes.

Here are also some basic recipes for lovely natural food colours to brighten the icing on the birthday cake.

Screwpine Leaves for Green Colouring

Screwpine (*pandan*) leaves *2, washed thoroughly*
Warm water *1–2 Tbsp*

1   Cut the leaves into short lengths, then place them in a blender or food processor and grind into a fine paste.

2   Place the paste into a bowl and mix with the warm water. Strain the liquid using a fine-mesh sieve.

3   Discard the residue. Add a few drops of the liquid to the basic butter icing to achieve a pale green colour.

Beetroot for Pink Colouring

Beetroot *1/2, peeled and cut into cubes*

1   Bring some water to the boil in a small pot. Add the beetroot cubes and cook for 15–20 minutes.

2   Remove the beetroot cubes, and allow the liquid to simmer. Reducing the liquid further will make for a deeper colour.

3   Allow the liquid to cool completely, then add a few drops to the basic butter icing to achieve a pink colour.

Saffron for Yellow Colouring

Saffron threads *5–10*

Hot water *1–2 tsp*

1 Soak saffron threads in 1–2 tsp hot water. Leave for 5–10 minutes to allow the colour to seep out from the saffron.

2 Discard the saffron threads. Add a few drops of the liquid to the basic butter icing to achieve a pale yellow colour.

Fruity Smoothie

Fruity Smoothie *Makes 1³/₄ cups*

Fresh strawberries *6, about 50 g (1³/₄ oz), washed, hulled and sliced*

Ripe banana *1, small, about 50 g (1³/₄ oz), peeled and chopped*

**Freshly-squeezed orange juice or store-bought
orange juice with no added sugar** *125 ml (4 fl oz / ¹/₂ cup)*

Whole milk *125 ml (4 fl oz / ¹/₂ cup)*

1   Place all the ingredients in a blender or food processor and blend to a smooth consistency.

2   Pour into cups and serve immediately.

Sweet Barley Dessert *Makes 3 cups*

Water *1.5 litres (48 fl oz / 6 cups)*

Barley *45 g (1¹/₂ oz / 1¹/₄ cup), washed and drained*

Bean curd sticks (fu chok) *30 g (1 oz), broken into small pieces*

Candied winter melon *25 g (⁴/₅ oz)*

1   Bring the water to the boil in a pot. Add all the ingredients and simmer over low heat for about 45 minutes or until the barley is soft.

2   Leave until dessert is just warm before serving.

※   Candied winter melon is traditionally used to sweeten Chinese desserts and can be found in most supermarkets.

※   These bean curd sticks are commonly referred to as *fu chok*. They are popularly used in Chinese desserts.

meal planner

	Anywhere between 4 and 6 months *Starting out*	Anywhere between 4 and 6 months *More established routine*
On waking	Milk feed	Milk feed
Breakfast	1–3 tsp iron-fortified commercial baby rice cereal Milk feed (as needed)*	1–3 tsp iron-fortified commercial baby rice cereal Milk feed (as needed)*
Mid morning	Milk feed	Milk feed
Lunch	Milk feed	2–3 Tbsp sweet potato purée 2–3 Tbsp apple purée Milk feed (as needed)*
Mid afternoon	Milk feed	Milk feed
Dinner	1–3 tsp iron-fortified commercial baby rice cereal Milk feed (as needed)*	1–3 tsp iron-fortified commercial baby rice cereal 2–3 Tbsp pea purée 2–3 Tbsp banana purée Milk feed (as needed)*
Supper	Milk feed	Milk feed

6 to 9 months	9 to 12 months	12 to 24 months
4–6 Tbsp banana ragi porridge Milk feed (as needed)*	1 whole wheat pancake roll, sliced 1/2 small banana Milk feed (as needed)*	1–2 slices French toast, sliced 1/2 cup milk
2–4 Tbsp fruit and yoghurt	3–4 Tbsp steamed tofu cubes with mango sauce	1/2 cup fruity smoothie
5–8 Tbsp fish and spinach porridge 2–4 Tbsp papaya purée Milk feed (as needed)*	6–10 Tbsp fine wheat noodles in broth 3–4 Tbsp watermelon cubes Milk feed (as needed)*	8–12 Tbsp baked macaroni with cheese and vegetables 1/4–1/3 cup melon cubes
2–4 Tbsp semolina surprise	2–4 Tbsp baked beetroot cubes	1 serving assorted fruit roll ups 1/2 cup milk
2–4 Tbsp plain rice porridge 2–4 Tbsp carrot and potato purée 2–3 Tbsp finely flaked fish 3–4 Tbsp apricot purée Milk feed (as needed)*	5–8 Tbsp alphabet pasta 3–4 Tbsp papaya cubes Milk feed (as needed)*	8–12 Tbsp cod with sweet corn sauce on rice 1/4–1/3 cup peach cubes
Milk feed	Milk feed	1/3 cup milk

frequently asked questions

Does my baby need extra water in addition to breastmilk or formula? No. Most healthy infants do not require additional water during the first six months, if they are exclusively breastfed. The exception is to offer a small amount of water in very hot weather, or if your baby is having severe diarrhoea or prolonged fever. Giving a lot of water in this early stage can interfere with adequate intake of milk. Before your child can take fluids from a cup, we feel the best strategy is to make water available in a bottle and to offer it to your baby as needed. After you introduce solids, you can begin to offer water in a cup in between and/or with meals. As your little one begins to include fluids like juice, porridge and soup, they also contribute water to his diet.

My baby seems to be teething. He is cranky and fussy and seems to be eating much less. Is this normal? Cutting the first tooth is indeed a milestone for every baby. The teething process usually starts anywhere between the ages of four and seven months. By the time your child turns three, he should have a full set of milk teeth. Teething can be very uncomfortable for baby. Yes, some babies are cranky, drool more and bite on anything they get their hands on. Some babies also run a slight fever and have diarrhoea during this period. To help your baby cope with the discomfort, you can give him a cool teething ring to bite on, or apply teething gel. Good oral hygiene will help your child grow up with a beautiful set of teeth. So, initiate the habit of cleaning your baby's mouth, well before the first tooth appears, by wiping his gums with a soft, moist cloth. Once more teeth erupt, teach your toddler to brush his teeth after meals.

Ever since I introduced solid food, my baby's poo has changed colour and it smells awful! Is there something wrong with him? No, this is normal. A variety of vegetables and some fruit can change the colour and smell of your baby's poo. If your baby is experiencing a lot of gas, diarrhoea or stomach upsets, talk to your baby's paediatrician or GP about it.

I am having problems producing enough breast milk. I am thinking of switching to formula instead, but I feel guilty and really want to breast feed longer. What can I do? This is a very common problem voiced by many Asian mothers. Often, the simplest way to increase your milk supply is to allow your baby to suckle longer and more frequently. Increased or more frequent breastfeeding also results in higher breast milk production. Suckling stimulates the let-down reflex that releases the flow of breast milk. This will also initiate one of the most successful breast feeding techniques called "feeding on demand". If your baby seems unsettled even after you have checked his diaper, considered wind/gas and tried to soothe him with rocking, it may be time for another feed. Expressing breast milk using a breast pump can also help increase supply, but letting your baby suckle is the most effective. So, it is a simple case of supply and demand! Also, relax and nourish yourself — eat well and drink enough fluids.

If you continue to have problems, seek the advice of a qualified lactation consultant who can help you and your baby. Most doctor's offices, clinics or hospitals will be able to refer you to one. If you are concerned that your baby is not feeding well or becoming dehydrated, seek your doctor's advice immediately.

There are some traditional beliefs about certain foods that will assist in increasing breast milk, such as papaya soup, black bean soup, fish soup, fenugreek, oatmeal, anise seed and alfalfa among many others. While the scientific proof is lacking, some mothers are convinced that these foods and herbs do help. As long as there is a history of long and safe use, traditional foods and herbs can be used to support a breast feeding mother as part of a well balanced diet.

Why do some milk products contain prebiotics and probiotics? Do I need to include these in my baby's diet? There are bacteria everywhere — some 'good' and some 'bad'. The 'bad' ones cause infections, but the friendly ones are protective to health. Scientists have discovered that 'good' bacteria, also called probiotics, reduce the number of bad bacteria in a child's digestive system. Breastfed babies tend to have a healthy amount of probiotics in their digestive system. This helps regulate bowel movements and reduce the incidence of constipation and diarrhoea. Prebiotics act like food for the friendly probiotic bacteria and this supports the healthy growth of good bacteria in the digestive system. That is why many food companies include probiotics and prebiotics in food products made for children and adults.

Can I warm up bottles of milk using the microwave oven? It is not recommended that you warm a bottle of milk in the microwave oven, since it heats unevenly causing "hot spots". This can cause scalding in your baby's mouth even if it feels fine. A bowl of hot water can warm a bottle evenly and safely. Always test the temperature of milk by pouring out a drop or two onto the surface of your hand or on the inside of your wrist. Milk should be just be at body temperature and not hot.

I heard that expensive fish like threadfin (*ikan kurau*), salmon and cod are the best types of fish for my baby. Do I always need to choose these types, and what are the health benefits of fish oils for my baby? Threadfin, salmon and cod are commonly chosen by mothers for their babies because they remain soft after cooking. In general, deep-sea fish like salmon and mackerel are a good sources of essential fatty acids, also known as EFAs. The body does not make these fats, so we need to get them from our diet. Of these EFAs, DHA plays an important role in brain and eye development of babies. While all fish contain some amounts of DHA, higher concentrations are found in herring, sardines and anchovies; a moderate amount in salmon; and a little less in sole, halibut, cod and shellfish. It is not necessary to choose these specific types of fish for your baby. Any white fish with a smooth texture including sea bass, snapper or garoupa will also provide protein, iron and EFAs needed for your baby's development.

My baby seems to cry all the time! It is so frustrating! Is this colic? What can I do about it? A word on colic. Science still has not completely figured it out! It is generally defined as periods of prolonged, inconsolable crying that seem to be caused by abdominal cramping and discomfort. It is most often seen in infants as young as two weeks of age but tends to disappear by three to four months. The most popular remedies involve soothing baby with rocking, walking, car rides, patting on the back, or playing soft music. In some cases, though still unproven, changing the breastfeeding mother's diet has been reported to help. The offenders are most likely to be cow's milk, wheat, peanuts, eggs or seafood. It is a case of trial and error, but if it keeps up, know that this is only a phase and it too, will pass.

My baby makes the funniest faces when I introduce new foods to her. Does that mean she doesn't like it and I should stop? Not necessarily. It is very common to get mixed reactions from children whether they like the new food or not. If your child puckers up her face, it does not always indicate dislike of food. She may simply be showing surprise at a new taste or texture of food. When babies push food out of their mouth, it may be a sign of an innate tongue extrusion reflex that has not yet disappeared or the fact that they have never experienced anything more than the consistency of breast milk before. If your baby still seems disinterested in the new food, stop and try again a few days later. It may take up to 10 tries before your baby learns to accept a new food.

How do I know that my nine month old baby has had enough to eat? One day she seems to eat very little and the next day she can eat amazing amounts! At any age, it is up to your child to decide when she has had enough to eat. That is one thing you cannot control! Once your child is hungry, she will eat. A good rule to remember is that you are a provider of good and nutritious food, but are not the food police. The best you can do is to provide appropriate amounts of a variety of healthy foods and the rest is up to her. Turning her head away, clamping her mouth shut and pushing the spoon away are likely signs that she is full or not hungry. It is best to step back and not force her to eat. She will eat again when she is ready, usually at the next meal or snack time. Force feeding your child, apart from not being recommended, can also foster the idea that cleaning your plate is best, where studies have shown that it may increase the risk of obesity.

I heard that adding infant cereal to milk when bottle feeding will help my baby sleep through the night. Is this true? No. This is a widely held belief, but there is not enough conclusive science to support this. Improved sleep patterns have more to do with developmental maturity and the baby's ability to comfort himself when awake in the absence of hunger, than it does with eating cereal. By giving cereal in a bottle, you are not teaching your baby about the mechanics or social skills of eating. There is also an increased risk of choking when giving the milk and rice cereal combo lying down in bed.

Can I put Chinese herbs or medicines in my baby's cereals or porridge? Many parents or grandparents believe that traditional Chinese herbs or medicines will help improve baby's appetite and digestive system. While some of these Chinese herbs or medicines, when used in small quantities, may not cause any harm to the baby, parents should exercise caution when choosing them for their baby. Always consult a qualified Traditional Chinese Medicine (TCM) physician for advice and buy only from reliable sources. If your baby needs medical attention, always remember to consult a medically-trained doctor. Chinese herbs and medicines should only play a supportive role.

know your child's daily nutrient goals

Ever wondered how many calories or how much of a particular nutrient your little one needs each day? The Dietary Reference Intake (DRI) will provide answers to your many questions.

Developed by the Food and Nutrition Board, Institute of Medicine, National Academies, USA, the DRI is a guide that provides a recommended daily dietary intake level for several nutrients that is sufficient to meet the requirement of nearly all healthy individuals in a particular life-stage and gender group. The DRIs reflect the best current scientific judgement on nutrient requirements for growth of children and the maintenance of good health. An individual can use it as a goal for usual intake, but bear in mind that these values are not absolute daily dietary requirements.

For your convenience, we have extracted some of the values for key nutrients for children between the ages of seven and 24 months. As a parent, you can refer to it when you want to compare the nutrients from a particular food, product or recipe to understand how it contributes to your child's overall nutrition. You can also add up the nutrient values of several foods to gauge the nutrient intake for a meal, snack or even your little one's intake for the whole day.

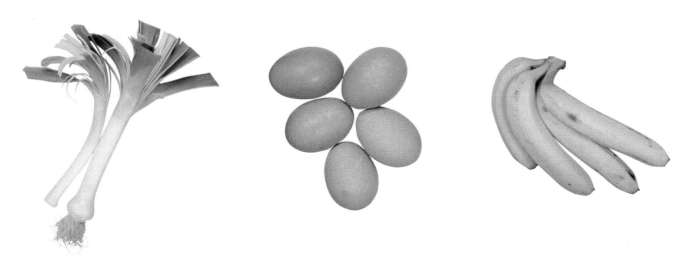

dietary reference intake (US)

AGE	WEIGHT RANGE* (KG)	ENERGY (KCAL)	PROTEIN (G)	CARBOHYDRATES (G)
7–12 mth	7.4–11.8	580–970	13.5	95
1–2 yr	9.6–14.2	774–1184	13.0	130

AGE	TOTAL FAT (G)	DIETARY FIBRE (G)	SODIUM (MG)	CALCIUM (MG)	IRON (MG)
7–12 mth	30	No data available	370	270	11.0
1–2 yr	26–53	19	1000	500	7.0

* *Average weight*

The table must not be used to treat or diagnose medical conditions or nutritional status. If you have any concerns about your child's nutritional intake, please talk to the attending paediatrician, GP or a dietitian.

You can find DRIs for other nutrients on the Food and Nutrition Board's website (http://www.iom.edu/CMS/3788/21370.aspx).

about the authors

Anna Jacob is a well-recognised dietitian and a highly-regarded speaker on food and nutrition topics in Singapore and throughout Southeast Asia. She is a founding partner and Director of Food & Nutrition Specialists Pte Ltd, providing consultancy services to a wide range of clients ranging from individuals, food and pharmaceutical companies as well as research, educational and health promotion organisations.

Anna loves creating healthier recipes with fresh foods and novel ingredients. Delicious, nutritious and easy-to-make recipes with a modern yet Asian slant are signature features of her creations. Over the years, Anna has created numerous innovative recipes for a variety of clients including leading food companies, retailers and magazines, and conducted cooking demonstrations. She has also fronted a television programme, *Breakfast On The Go*, on Singapore MediaCorp's Channel NewsAsia.

A long-standing member of the Singapore Nutrition and Dietetic Association (SNDA), Anna has served actively on SNDA's main committee. She was the editor of the SNDA journal for 11 years, and served as the association's president for two years.

Anna received her Bachelor's degree in Nutrition and Dietetics and her Master's degree in Food Service Management and Dietetics from the Women's Christian College, Madras University, India.

Pauline Chan is a dietitian with broad professional experience through her work in the USA and Southeast Asia. She began her career as a clinical dietitian in hospitals, specialising in renal, pediatric, enteral and parenteral nutrition in the USA. Currently a partner and director of Food & Nutrition Specialists Pte Ltd, Pauline provides a range of nutritional services for individuals, government and corporate organisations, including menu planning and recipe development.

Pauline is also a frequent resource speaker for public forums, conferences and seminars in Singapore and the region. A dynamic speaker fluent in English and several Chinese dialects, she has participated in many Chinese television and radio programmes to communicate nutrition information to the public. She also conducted cooking demonstrations and fronted a television programme, *Breakfast On The Go*, with Anna Jacob on Singapore MediaCorp's Channel NewsAsia.

An active member of the SNDA, Pauline also serves on its main committee, and is a registered dietitian (RD) with the American Dietetic Association. Pauline received her Bachelor's degree in Chemistry from the Chinese University of Hong Kong and her Master's degree in Nutrition and Dietetics from New York University, USA.

Samantha Thiessen is a dietitian licensed by the College of Dietitians of Ontario (Canada) as well as a member of the Dietitians of Canada. While based Singapore, Samantha worked as part of the team of dietitians and nutritionists at Food & Nutrition Specialists Pte Ltd, engaging in a variety of responsibilities including working with individuals, groups and corporations. She was also a member of the SNDA. Samantha currently resides in Canada.

Samantha graduated with a Bachelor of Applied Science degree in Food and Nutrition from the Ryerson University, Toronto, Canada and completed a dietetic internship in Canada before working as a clinical dietitian in both community and hospital settings.

Wong Yuefen is a dietitian at Food & Nutrition Specialists Pte Ltd, where she helps develop childhood nutrition and school health programmes. She also provides dietetic and nutrition consultancy services to corporate clients, as well as residents in hospitals and nursing homes. Her interests include the prevention of childhood obesity through healthier eating habits, and she has developed web-based games and nutrition education resource materials for school children. She is also interested in exploring the efficacy of pre- and probiotics in addressing conditions such as irritable bowel syndrome.

Yuefen received her Diploma in Applied Food Science and Nutrition from Temasek Polytechnic, Singapore and her Bachelor's degree in Nutrition & Dietetics from Flinders University of South Australia, Adelaide, Australia. She is a registered dietitian with the Dietetic Association of Australia, and a member of the SNDA.

Janie Chua is a dietitian at Food & Nutrition Specialists Pte Ltd, where her key responsibilities include the development and facilitation of workplace health promotion programmes, ranging from cafeteria assessment to staff nutrition education activities. She is also actively involved in nutrition education programmes targeted at school children, working closely with the Health Promotion Board, Singapore, as well as directly with schools. As a dietitian, Janie also provides dietetic counselling and advice to residents of hospitals and nursing homes. She particularly enjoys caring for her patients and developing personalised meal plans to suit their individual nutritional requirements.

Janie received her Diploma in Applied Food Science and Nutrition from Temasek Polytechnic, Singapore and her Bachelor's degree in Nutrition & Dietetics from Flinders University of South Australia, Adelaide, Australia. She is a registered dietitian with the Dietetic Association of Australia, and a member of the SNDA.

resource list

Alexander, Lynn & Yeong Boon Yee. *Feed Your Child Right*. 2002. Times Books International.

American Academy of Pediatrics. *Pediatric Nutrition Handbook*. 1998.

American Academy of Pediatrics. *The Official, Complete Home Reference Guide to Your Child's Nutrition*. 1999. Dietz, W. & Stern, L. (editors). Villard.

American Dietetic Association & Dietitians of Canada Manual of Clinical Dietetics, 6th Edition, 2000.

American Dietetic Association. *Food Allergies: Tips from the Nutrition Experts*. 1998. John Wiley & Sons, Inc.

Birch, L. *Development of food acceptance patterns in the first years of life*. Proceedings of the Nutrition Society, 57:617–624, 1998.

Children, Youth and Women's Health website, *Parenting and Child Health*. South Australia. http://www.cyh.com/HealthTopics/HealthTopicCategories.aspx?&p=302

Dubois L, Girard M. *Early determinants of overweight at 4.5 years in a population-based longitudinal study*. Int J Obes (Lond). 2006 Apr; 30(4):610–7.

Eisenberg, A., Murkoff, H, and Hathaway, S. *What to Expect The First Year*. 1989. Workman Publishing.

Friedman N.J., Zeiger R.S., *The role of breast-feeding in the development of allergies and asthma*. J Allergy Clin Immunil. 2005 Jun;115(6):1238–48.

Harder T., Bergmann R., Kallischnigg G., Plagemann A. *Duration of breastfeeding and risk of overweight: A meta-analysis*. Am J Epidemiol. 2005 Sep 1;162(5):397–403.

Hawes, Gerrie. *Feed me!* 2005. Kyle Cathie Ltd.

Health Promotion Board, Singapore website. http://www.hpb.gov.sg

Innis S.M., *Trans fatty intakes during pregnancy, infancy and early childhood.* Atheroscler Suppl. 2006 May; 7(2):17–20.

Irwin, Joseph J., Kirchner, Jeffrey T. *Anemia in Children.* American Family Physician. 2001; 64:1379–86.

Journal of the American Dietetic Association. Feeding Infants and Toddlers Study (FITS) 2002 results. January 2006 Supplement 1. Elsevier.

Karmel, Annabel. *Feeding Your Baby & Toddler.* 2004. Dorling Kindersley.

Kimmel, Martha & David. *Mummy Made: Home Cooking For a Healthy Baby & Toddler.* 2000. Bantam Books.

Medline Encyclopedia. http://www.nlm.nih.gov/medlineplus/encyclopedia.html

National Institute of Health website. http://ods.od.nih.gov

United States Food and Drug Administration (US FDA) *What You Need to Know About Mercury in Fish and Shellfish.* http://www.cfsan.fda.gov/~dms/admehg3.html

World Health Organization. *Complementary Feeding of Young Children in Developing Countries: A Review of Current Scientific Knowledge.* 1998.

World Health Organization. *Complementary Feeding. Report of the Global Consultation.* Geneva, 2001.

recipe index